A JUMPIN' JIM'S UKULELE SONGBOOK

The DAILY UKULELE
BARITONE EDITION

365 Songs For Better Living
FOR BARITONE UKULELE

COMPILED AND ARRANGED BY
LIZ AND JIM BELOFF

Copyright @ 2013 FLEA MARKET MUSIC, INC.

7777 W. BLUEMOUND RD. P.O. BOX 13819 MILWAUKEE, WI 53213

Edited by Ronny S. Schiff
Cover and Art Direction by Elizabeth Maihock Beloff
Graphics and Music Typography by Charylu Roberts
Illustrations by Pete McDonnell

Contents

Foreword	3
Song Index	4–5
Ukulele 101	6–7
How To Use This Book	8–9
Some Chord Alternatives And Shortcuts	10–11
Chord Chart	12
Songs	13–333
Songs For Holidays And Celebrations	285–310
Songs For Children	311–333
Your Notes Here	334–335
Acknowledgements And Bio	336

Also available: (Songbooks) *Jumpin' Jim's Ukulele Favorites; Jumpin' Jim's Ukulele Tips 'n' Tunes; Jumpin' Jim's Ukulele Gems; Jumpin' Jim's Ukulele Christmas; Jumpin' Jim's '60s Uke-In; Jumpin' Jim's Gone Hawaiian; Jumpin' Jim's Camp Ukulele; Jumpin' Jim's Ukulele Masters: Lyle Ritz; Jumpin' Jim's Ukulele Beach Party; Jumpin' Jim's Ukulele Masters: Herb Ohta; Jumpin' Jim's Ukulele Masters: Lyle Ritz Solos; Jumpin' Jim's Ukulele Spirit; Jumpin' Jim's Gone Hollywood; Jumpin' Jim's Ukulele Island; Jumpin' Jim's Ukulele Masters: John King—The Classical Ukulele; Jumpin' Jim's Ukulele Country; Jumpin' Jim's The Bari Best; Ukulele Fretboard Roadmaps (with Fred Sokolow); Jumpin' Jim's Happy Holidays; Jumpin' Jim's Ukulele Masters: Lyle Lite; Blues Ukulele; Bluegrass Ukulele; From Lute To Uke; The Daily Ukulele; The Baroque Ukulele; The Daily Ukulele: Leap Year Edition.*
(Pictorial History) *The Ukulele: A Visual History.*

Foreword

Along with an apple a day, a daily allowance of vitamins and minerals and a daily constitutional...playing music regularly is one of the healthiest lifestyle habits you can practice. It makes you smarter. It makes you laugh. And it even has romantic advantages. For those of you who have played a musical instrument, or total beginners who have always longed to play, this book, along with a ukulele, is your key to musical health and happiness. In *The Daily Ukulele: Baritone Edition,* you'll find easy arrangements of hundreds of great, time-tested tunes at your fingertips.

One thing we've learned in all of our years of publishing ukulele songbooks is that the uke is a very social musical instrument. This would explain the growth of ukulele clubs throughout the United States, and the rest of the world. It's a good bet that at any given moment somewhere on the planet a group of players is gathered together having a great time strumming and singing a bunch of favorite songs.

Part of this is due to the modest nature of the ukulele. Although the uke has always attracted its fair share of virtuosos, most players are perfectly happy to use it as an accompaniment to a song. And when groups of like-minded strummers gather, it can be a memorable experience. For those who have visited a well-established ukulele club, it can seem like a cross between a secret society gathering and a tent revival. Typically, these clubs create their own culture and traditions with regular meetings, special events and gigs, guest performances, and sometimes even annual festivals. At the center of it all are the songs the members are passionate about playing and singing together.

We created *The Daily Ukulele* with these songs in mind. The idea was to pull together 365 well-known songs with easy arrangements in uke-friendly keys that are especially fun to play and sing with others or on your own. Everything from Stephen Foster to Irving Berlin, The Beatles and Bob Dylan, kids songs, gospel songs, Christmas carols, Broadway and Hollywood tunes and even a couple of tributes to the ukulele. And, all bound together in one convenient volume.

This particular edition of *The Daily Ukulele* is specifically arranged for those playing baritone ukuleles tuned down to DGBE (G tuning). Here, all the songs are in the same keys as the GCEA-tuned edition but with the chord frames changed to reflect baritone ukulele chord fingerings. All of the "First Note" grids have been changed as well to show where the initial note of the melody can be found on the baritone fingerboard. As a result, this should make it easier and more fun for baritone uke fans to play from *The Daily Ukulele* along with C-tuned uke players.

Over the years we've seen many worn copies of our other *Jumpin' Jim's* songbooks. We take special pride in seeing these especially "loved" copies because they clearly have been enjoyed. Here's hoping that this copy of *The Daily Ukulele: Baritone Edition,* will become just as "loved."

Keep on strummin',

Liz and Jim Beloff
Clinton, CT
2013

Song Index

SONG	PAGE
After You've Gone	14
Ain't Misbehavin'	15
Ain't She Sweet	16
Ain't We Got Fun?	17
All I Have To Do Is Dream	18
All My Loving	19
All Night, All Day	312
All Of Me	20
All Through The Night	312
Aloha 'Oe	21
Alphabet Song	313
Always	22
Amazing Grace	21
America (My Country 'Tis Of Thee)	23
America, The Beautiful	23
Anchors Aweigh	24
Anniversary Song	290
Any Time	25
Are You Lonesome Tonight?	13
Around The World	26
Auld Lang Syne	286
Avalon	27
Away In A Manger	296
Baa, Baa, Black Sheep	313
Baby Face	31
Baby Love	28
Baby, Won't You Please Come Home	29
Bad, Bad Leroy Brown	30
Battle Hymn Of The Republic, The	32
Bear Went Over The Mountain, The	314
Beautiful Brown Eyes	34
Beautiful Dreamer	33
Best Things In Life Are Free, The	34
Bill Bailey, Won't You Please Come Home	35
Blowin' In The Wind	36
Blue Christmas	297
Blue Hawaii	37
Blue Skies	38
Brahms' Lullaby	314
Brown Eyed Girl	39
Buffalo Gals (Won't You Come Out Tonight)	40
By The Beautiful Sea	42
By The Light Of The Silvery Moon	43
Bye Bye Blackbird	40
Bye Bye Blues	38
Bye Bye Love	41
Cabaret	44
Caissons Go Rolling Along, The	45
California Dreamin'	46
California, Here I Come	47
Can't Buy Me Love	48
Can't Help But Smile	50
Can't Help Falling In Love	51
Candy Man, The	315
Careless Love	49
Carolina In The Morning	52
Chapel Of Love	53
Chicago (That Toddlin' Town)	54
Chinatown, My Chinatown	55
Chipmunk Song, The	298
Cindy	55
Clementine	51
(They Long To Be) Close To You	56
Come And Go With Me	43
Consider Yourself	57
Crazy	58
Danny Boy	59
Daydream	60
Daydream Believer	62
Deck The Halls	299
Deep In The Heart Of Texas	64
Devoted To You	63
Dinah	61
Dixie Land	65
Do Lord	65
Don't Be Cruel (To A Heart That's True)	66
Don't Get Around Much Anymore	68
Don't Worry, Be Happy	70
Do-Re-Mi	316
Down By The Riverside	67
Down In The Valley	69
Downtown	72
Dream A Little Dream Of Me	69
Dreidel Song, The	294
Drunken Sailor, The	71
Easter Parade	289
Edelweiss	75
Eensy Weensy Spider	317
Eight Days A Week	74
Enjoy Yourself (It's Later Than You Think)	76
Erie Canal, The	77
Ev'ry Time I Feel The Spirit	73
Everybody Loves Somebody	78
Far Away Places	79
Farmer In The Dell, The	317
Feliz Navidad	300
Fields Of Gold	80
59th Street Bridge Song, The (Feelin' Groovy)	97
First Noel, The	301
Five Foot Two, Eyes Of Blue (Has Anybody Seen My Gal?)	82
Folsom Prison Blues	83
For He's A Jolly Good Fellow	81
For Me And My Gal	84
From Me To You	86
Funiculì, Funiculà	85
Georgia On My Mind	87
Getting To Know You	88
Give Me That Old Time Religion	90
Give My Regards To Broadway	89
Glory Of Love, The	90
Glow-Worm, The	95
Go Down, Moses	91
Go Tell It On The Mountain	299
Good Day Sunshine	92
Good Morning To All	319
Good Night	93
Goodnight, Irene	94
Good Night Ladies	95
Groovy Kind Of Love, A	96
Happy Together	98
Happy Trails	99
Hard Day's Night, A	100
Hard Times Come Again No More	101
Hark! The Herald Angels Sing	302
Hava Nagila	295
Hawaii Ponoi	103
Hawaiian Wedding Song, The	102
Heart And Soul	104
Hello, Dolly!	105
Help!	106
He's Got The Whole World In His Hands	107
Hey, Good Lookin'	108
Hey Jude	109
Home On The Range	110
Hound Dog	111
How Can I Keep From Singing?	112
How Can You Mend A Broken Heart	113
How Sweet It Is (To Be Loved By You)	114
Hukilau Song, The	115
Hush, Little Baby	318
I Ain't Got Nobody (And Nobody Cares For Me)	116
I Can't Give You Anything But Love	117
I Feel Fine	118
If I Had A Hammer	119
If You're Happy And You Know It	318
I Left My Heart In San Francisco	120
I'll Be Seeing You	121
I'll Fly Away	124
I'll Follow The Sun	122
I'm A Believer	123
Imagine	125
I'm Always Chasing Rainbows	126
I'm Beginning To See The Light	127
I'm Henry VIII, I Am!	128
Indiana	129
In The Good Old Summertime	131
In The Sweet By And By	124
I Saw Her Standing There	130
I Saw The Light	132
It's A Small World	319
It's My Party	137
It's Only A Paper Moon	133
I've Been Working On The Railroad	134
I've Just Seen A Face	135
I Walk The Line	138
I Want To Hold Your Hand	136
Jackson	139
Ja-Da	138
Jambalaya (On The Bayou)	140
Jingle-Bell Rock	304
Jingle Bells	305
Joshua Fought The Battle Of Jericho	141
Joy To The World	303
Joyful, Joyful, We Adore Thee	141
Keep On The Sunny Side	142
King Of The Road	143
Kumbaya	142
Last Train To Clarksville	144
Let It Be	146
Let It Be Me	147
Let It Snow! Let It Snow! Let It Snow!	306

Title	Page
Let Me Call You Sweetheart	145
Let's Get Together	148
Letter, The	149
Let The Rest Of The World Go By	150
Limehouse Blues	151
Loch Lomond	145
Long, Long Ago	152
Look For The Silver Lining	153
Love Me Do	154
Love Me Tender	154
Love Potion Number 9	155
Lovely Hula Hands	156
Makin' Whoopee!	157
Marine's Hymn, The	159
Mary Had A Little Lamb	320
Me and Bobby McGee	158
Mele Kalikimaka	307
Michael, Row The Boat Ashore	161
Mickey Mouse March	321
Midnight Special	160
Miss The Mississippi And You	162
Mister Sandman	161
Moon River	163
Moonlight Bay	165
More We Get Together, The	320
My Blue Heaven	169
My Bonnie (Lies Over The Ocean)	167
My Favorite Things	164
My Funny Valentine	287
My Girl	166
My Guy	168
My Love	170
My Old Kentucky Home	171
Night Before, The	172
Nobody Knows The Trouble I've Seen	173
Ob-La-Di, Ob-La-Da	174
O Come, All Ye Faithful	308
Oh, Babe, What Would You Say?	176
Oh, Susanna	178
Oh, What A Beautiful Mornin'	177
Oh Where, Oh Where Has My Little Dog Gone?	321
Old Folks At Home (Swanee River)	179
Old MacDonald Had A Farm	323
On A Slow Boat To China	180
On Broadway	181
On The Beach At Waikiki	184
On The Good Ship Lollipop	322
On The Road Again	182
On The Sunny Side Of The Street	183
On Top Of Old Smoky	184
Over The River And Through The Woods	292
Peace Like A River	185
Pearly Shells	186
Peggy Sue	187
Pennies From Heaven	188
Please Please Me	189
Polly Wolly Doodle	323
Pomp And Circumstance	291
Prayer Of Thanksgiving	293
Princess Poo-Poo-ly Has Plenty Pa-Pa-Ya	190
Proud Mary	191
Que Sera, Sera (Whatever Will Be, Will Be)	192
Rainbow Connection, The	324
Raindrops Keep Fallin' On My Head	193
Rawhide	194
Red River Valley	195
Red Rubber Ball	196
Ring Of Fire	197
Rock-A My Soul	201
Rock Around The Clock	198
Rocky Top	199
Row, Row, Row Your Boat	325
Rudolph The Red-Nosed Reindeer	309
Runaway	200
Runnin' Wild	201
Sakura (Cherry Blossoms)	210
Save The Last Dance For Me	202
Second Hand Rose	203
Seems Like Old Times	204
Sentimental Journey	205
Shall We Gather At The River	208
She'll Be Comin' 'Round The Mountain	209
She Loves You	206
Shenandoah	208
Shine On, Harvest Moon	209
Side By Side	210
Sidewalks Of New York	211
Silent Night	308
Simple Gifts	211
Sing	212
Sixteen Tons	213
Skip To My Lou	325
Sloop John B., The	214
Smiles	215
Some Folks	216
Some Of These Days	217
Song Of The Islands	214
Song Sung Blue	218
Spoonful Of Sugar, A	326
Stand By Me	219
Star Spangled Banner, The	221
Strangers In The Night	220
Sunny Afternoon	222
Sunrise, Sunset	224
Supercalifragilisticexpialidocious	327
Surfin' U.S.A.	223
Swanee	225
Swing Low, Sweet Chariot	226
Take Me Out To The Ballgame	227
Taps	227
Tell Me Why	226
That Hawaiian Melody	228
That's Amoré (That's Love)	229
That'll Be The Day	230
There Is A Tavern In The Town	236
There's A Kind Of Hush	231
These Boots Are Made For Walkin'	232
This Land Is Your Land	234
This Little Light Of Mine	235
This Old Man	328
This Train	236
Those Were The Days	238
Three Blind Mice	329
Three Little Birds	237
Tie Me Kangaroo Down Sport	240
Times They Are A-Changin', The	239
Tiny Bubbles	241
Tonight You Belong To Me	242
Too-Ra-Loo-Ra-Loo-Ral (That's An Irish Melody)	288
Toot, Toot, Tootsie! (Good-bye!)	243
To You, Sweetheart, Aloha	248
Try To Remember	244
Turn! Turn! Turn! (To Everything There Is A Season)	246
26 Miles (Santa Catalina)	233
Twinkle, Twinkle Little Star	331
Ukulele Lady	249
Ukuleles Are The Best	248
Unchained Melody	247
Under The Boardwalk	245
Up On The Roof	250
Upside Down	330
Wabash Cannon Ball, The	251
Wade In The Water	252
Wake Up Little Susie	253
Walk Right In	255
Walkin' My Baby Back Home	254
Waltzing Matilda	256
Water Is Wide, The	252
Wayfaring Stranger	255
We'll Meet Again	259
We Shall Overcome	257
We Three Kings Of Orient Are	310
We Wish You A Merry Christmas	310
What A Wonderful World	260
What'll I Do?	258
When I Fall In Love	261
When I'm Sixty-Four	262
When Irish Eyes Are Smiling	288
When the Red, Red Robin Comes Bob, Bob Bobbin' Along	264
When The Saints Go Marching In	267
When You Wish Upon A Star	266
When You're Smiling (The Whole World Smiles With You)	265
Whispering	267
White Sport Coat, A (And A Pink Carnation)	268
Why Do Fools Fall In Love?	269
Wildwood Flower	270
Will The Circle Be Unbroken	270
With A Little Help From My Friends	272
World Is Waiting For the Sunrise, The	273
World Without Love	271
Wouldn't It Be Loverly	274
Wouldn't It Be Nice	275
Yankee Doodle Boy	291
Yellow Rose Of Texas, The	276
Yellow Submarine	277
Yes Sir, That's My Baby	278
You Are My Sunshine	279
You Made Me Love You (I Didn't Want To Do It)	280
Your Cheatin' Heart	281
You're A Grand Old Flag	282
You're Nobody 'Til Somebody Loves You	284
You've Got A Friend In Me	332
You've Got To Hide Your Love Away	283
Zip-A-Dee-Doo-Dah	333

Ukulele 101

The songs in this book are arranged for baritone ukuleles in G tuning. In this tuning, the individual strings from the top (closest to your nose) to bottom (closest to your toes) are tuned DGBE. A lot of chords can be made with one or two fingers and many of the songs in this book require six chords or less.

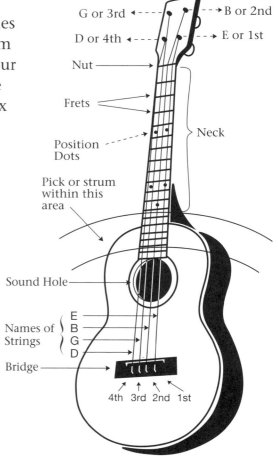

Uke G Tuning

One easy way to tune a ukulele is with a pitchpipe or electronic tuner matching the strings with the notes.

Here are the notes on the piano:

Keeping In Tune

Many ukuleles have friction tuners that include a small screw at the end of the tuner. The secret to staying in tune is to keep these screws tight enough so that the tuners don't slip, but loose enough that the tuners still turn.

Holding The Uke

Press your uke against your body about 3/4ths of the way up your forearm. Your strumming hand should naturally fall on top of the upper frets (not over the soundhole). Hold the neck of the uke between your thumb and first finger of your other hand, so that your fingers are free to move about the fretboard.

Making The Chords

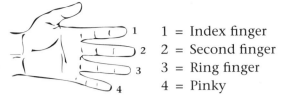

You make chords by putting various combinations of fingers on the fretboard. In this songbook you'll find chord diagrams that show where to put your fingers to make the right sound. The vertical lines in the diagrams represent strings and the horizontal lines represent the frets. The numbers at the bottom of the chords shown below indicate what fingers to use.

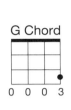  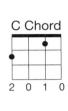 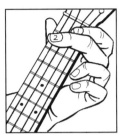  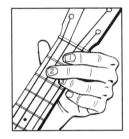

Remember:
1. When pressing down the strings, use the tips of your fingers.
2. Always press down in the space between the frets, not on them.
3. Press the strings down to the fretboard. If you hear a buzz it may be because you are not pressing hard enough or are too close to a fret.
4. Keep your thumb at the back of the neck, parallel to the frets.

Making The Strums

The Common Strum: This is the most basic up/down strum. It can be produced solely with your index finger going down the strings with your fingernail and up with the cushion of your fingertip. You can also try this with the pad of your thumb running down the strings and the tip of your index finger going up. This strum will work fine on most of the songs in this book. A good example would be "King Of The Road."

Waltz Strum: This ¾ rhythm can be produced simply with your thumb or index finger in sets of three down strums. You can use this on ¾ songs like "Are You Lonesome Tonight?" and "Around The World."

Island Strum: This lilting, syncopated strum is a combination of quick up and down strums plus a roll. In a typical 4-beat measure it would look like this:

⊓ = downstroke

v = upstroke

⊓   roll v   v   ⊓   v

One and **Two** and **Three** and **Four** and…

Here's how to make the roll strum.

Play the downstroke with your thumb and the upstroke with your index finger. The roll is made by running the ring, middle and index fingers quickly in succession across the strings. Ideal songs to use this on are "Under The Boardwalk" or "Up On The Roof."

Tremolo: This is used often as an ending flourish for a song. It's produced by running your index finger across the strings rapidly. If you are performing, this will suggest to your audience that you are finishing the song and they should get ready to applaud. Try this at the end of any song where you want a "big finish."

How To Use This Book

The best way to use this songbook is, well, daily. Because there are 365 songs, you can play a different song each day for a whole year. (You get one day off during a leap year!) The songs are not always in strict alphabetical order, so consult the index in front when in doubt. We did create two special sections: The first is "Songs For Holidays And Celebrations," where you'll find Christmas carols and other holiday-related material. This section is organized around the calendar year starting with "Auld Lang Syne" for New Year's Eve. The other special section is "Songs For Children," which are tunes that are appropriate for kids to play or parents who want to play for their children.

Many of the songs included here should be easy for you to play and sing right away. Here are a few things to note that will make this songbook especially enjoyable:

1. **Chord Grids**: Just in case you need a reminder of how to make a certain chord, the chord grids for each song are directly under the title, in order of their appearance. The *Chord Chart* on page 12 shows suggested fingerings.

2. **First Note**: This shows the first singing note of the song. Although many of the first notes in this book are below middle C, all are above D below middle C, which is the lowest note on a DGBE-tuned baritone ukulele. This means that every single starting pitch is represented in the first note grid. In some songs, that note is fairly high up on the E string like the C on the 8th fret. In this case, rather than extend the "First Note" grid to 8 lines, we simply put an "8" next to the dot to indicate that the starting pitch can be found on the 8th fret of that string.

3. **Instrumentals**: There are a few songs included here that have instrumental sections built into the arrangement. An example of this is in "How Sweet It Is." You are welcome to ignore these sections entirely or take a real solo. Often solo uke performers will make a trumpet or trombone sound with their mouths. Harmonicas and kazoos will work here, too.

4. **N.C.**: Whenever you see N.C. above the staff that means "no chord," a place in the song where you should stop playing until you get to the next chord. This "break" can be a nice flourish that will add drama to your performance. A well-known example is in the sixth line of "Five Foot Two, Eyes Of Blue."

There are some additional symbols that you'll see used throughout the arrangements in this songbook. We've listed a few below with their meanings:

‖: :‖ Repeat Signs: These mean that the section within the signs should be performed again before going on to the next section.

First Ending: Play through the measures under this bracketed area and then go back to the beginning of that section. Then look for further endings.

***D.C.* Da Capo**: This means "from the beginning," indicating to go back to the beginning of the music.

***D.S.* Dal Segno**: Means to look for the 𝄋 sign and repeat that section from the sign.

⊕ Coda: Ending section. When you see "*To Coda* ⊕," jump ahead to the closing section that begins with this symbol.

The Arrangements

Over the years of publishing our *Jumpin' Jim's* songbooks, we've fine-tuned our approach to arranging songs for the ukulele. Often it's a careful balancing act between finding a uke-friendly playing key while also keeping the melody in a comfortable singing range. For *The Daily Ukulele* we had an additional goal of keeping the arrangements as streamlined as possible.

Because all of the songs here are in the same keys as the original *Daily Ukulele*, you'll find most of the songs in C, F and G and some in D and A. Those keys are fairly easy for G-tuned ukuleles with the exception of F, which almost always includes F and B♭, two of the more challenging chords on a baritone ukulele. Because the whole point of this book is to allow both C-tuned and G-tuned ukes to play together we had no choice but to leave the keys as they were. The upside of this is that you will have many opportunities to perfect your F and B♭ shapes by playing through this book.

Transposing

Aside from the challenges of F and B♭, we hope most of the songs in this book will be in keys that are easy for you to play *and* sing. In case a particular song feels too high or too low, you have the option of transposing it to a more comfortable key. If the song is in F and is a bit too challenging, try going up to G and raising the chords a whole step. That would mean, for example, that F would become G, B♭ would become C and C7 would become D7. With a bit of experience, you should be able to do this in real time, while you are playing the song in tempo. The same would apply for transposing songs from A down to G or D down to C. If the song still feels too high or low, you may want to try a more dramatic transposition, like G to C or F to C and vice versa.

With some experience, you'll become very familiar with the chords that typically appear in uke-friendly keys and will be transposing easily and quickly from one key to the next. This is especially true for simpler songs with a minimum of chords like blues and many kids' and folk tunes. The transposition chart below will help you keep track of the essential chords in the most uke-friendly keys:

Chords in	C	F	G7	Am	Dm	E7
D	D	G	A7	Bm	Em	F♯7
F	F	B♭	C7	Dm	Gm	A7
G	G	C	D7	Em	Am	B7
A	A	D	E7	F♯m	Bm	C♯7

For example, if you wish to transpose a song in the key of C to the key of D, you would

	The Original Chord		The New Chord
Change	C	to	D
Change	F	to	G
Change	G7	to	A7
Change	Am	to	Bm
Change	Dm	to	Em
Change	E7	to	F♯7

In this case, everything moves up one whole step.

Some Chord Alternatives And Shortcuts

The Hawaiian A7

The traditional baritone A7 chord is made by placing your index finger (or middle finger) across all four strings of the second fret, and then putting your middle finger (or ring finger) on the third fret of the E string. There is an alternative A7 that is made by putting your middle finger on the second fret of the D string and ring finger on the second fret of the B string. (On a GCEA-tuned ukulele, this fingering is a D7 chord and because the two-fingered form is popular in Hawaii, it is often known as the "Hawaiian D7.") Besides being easier to play, the two-fingered bari A7 has a more open and mellower sound. While we decided to show the traditional form throughout the book, you are welcome to use the easier two-fingered version and may find you prefer it on certain songs.

Barred A7 Chord   Two-Finger "Hawaiian" A7 Chord

The Challenging F Chord

For new bari uke players, the F is one of the more challenging chords to make. Typically, you make an F by holding down the first frets of both the E and B strings with your index finger; then putting your middle finger on the second fret of the G string and your ring finger on the third fret of the D string. A strong squeeze between your fingers and your thumb is recommended to make a clean-sounding F without any string buzz.

One alternative is to barre the chord. This means laying your index finger down across all the strings on the first fret while adding the middle and ring finger as described previously. For some, stretching the index finger across four strings is easier than holding down two strings with the first joint. (It's also good to practice making these barre chords as often as possible, since they will open up numerous chord possibilities further up the fretboard.) Another even simpler solution is to play the F, but leave the top D string open so that it looks like you're playing a Dm7. Not having to stretch your hand to the D string makes the chord easier to produce. However, you need to be careful not to strum the D string, only the top three strings. If you accidentally strum the D string, the chord will sound odd, not like an F. This alternative is especially appropriate when you just need to play an F chord for only a brief time (a measure or less).

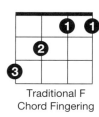 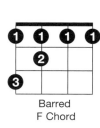 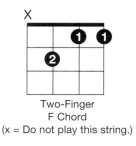

Traditional F Chord Fingering   Barred F Chord   Two-Finger F Chord (x = Do not play this string.)

The Dramatic Diminished Chord

You'll find a lot of diminished chords in this book. Most can be found in the older Tin-Pan Alley songs like "For Me And My Gal." These chords have a unique, dramatic personality and are especially prominent in the soundtracks of early black and white short films. Most players use all four fingers to make these chords, but they can be barred as well. If you barre the chord with your index finger, you can use your middle and ring finger to cover the remaining notes and, thus, avoid using your little finger. Another easier option is to play a D7 chord shape in the same place that calls for a four-finger diminished chord. As long as you only strum the top three strings, it will sound okay, especially if you're only using the chord for a measure or less.

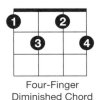
Four-Finger
Diminished Chord

Barred Three-Finger
Diminished Chord

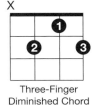
Three-Finger
Diminished Chord
(x = Do not play this string.)

The Pinky D

Most baritone ukulele instruction books recommend playing a D chord with the index, middle and ring fingers. This allows the new player to avoid having to use their weakest finger—the pinky. This is okay to start playing quickly, but it's not very efficient when moving from a D chord to a D7, which is a common transition. In order to do that, all three fingers need to lift and regroup to make the D7. If, on the other hand, the D is made with the middle finger on the second fret of the G string, the ring finger on the second fret of the E string and pinky on the third fret of the B string you need only lift the pinky and place the index finger on the first fret of the B string to make the same transition. See the beginning of "Home On The Range" to try this out.

Non-Pinky
D Chord

Pinky D

The Baritone Cmaj7

There are a handful of songs in this book that employ the Cmaj7. On a GCEA-tuned ukulele, the Cmaj7 is a very easy chord to make, requiring just one finger on the second fret of the A string. On the baritone uke, the first-position version of a Cmaj7 is 2,4,1,3, which requires a good deal of finger stretching to produce. The second position Cmaj7 is a barre chord (5,5,5,7), and is a bit easier to finger. Hopping up to the 5th fret to make the second-position Cmaj7 can be awkward, however, and sometimes the chord sounds out of place with other first-position chords. In a few select places, an alternate Cmaj7 (2,0,0,3) is employed, which is easy to make but is missing the root (C). In these cases (like "Que Sera, Sera"), the ease of fingering trumped the need for the fuller chord. One final variation is 5,5,0,0, which can sound a bit muddy on the bari, but sounds great on "Close To You." Here are the four variations:

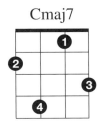
Cmaj7

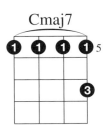
Cmaj7

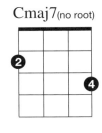
Cmaj7 (no root)

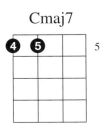
Cmaj7

The Baritone Em7

Those who carefully compare the chord names in this book to the GCEA edition will note one significant alteration. Where there is a call for an Em7, in most cases the chord has been changed to Em in this book. This is because Em7 on a baritone ukulele is often made with all strings played open (without any fingers). All open strings can sound rather muddy and unanchored on a bari while a regular Em, with the addition of the low E on the second fret of the D string, can make the chord sound much richer.

Em7

Em

Chord Chart

Tune Ukulele
D G B E

Major Chords

A, A♯ B♭, B, C, C♯ D♭, D, D♯ E♭, E, F, F♯ G♭, G, G♯ A♭

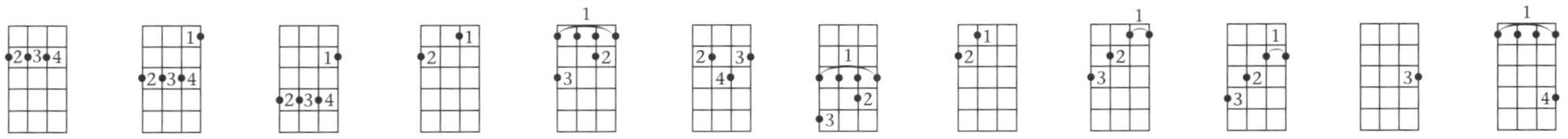

Minor Chords

Am, A♯m B♭m, Bm, Cm, C♯m D♭m, Dm, D♯m E♭m, Em, Fm, F♯m G♭m, Gm, G♯m A♭m

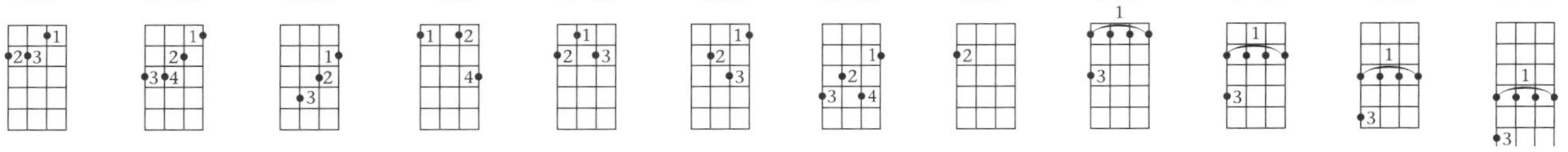

Dominant Seventh Chords

A7, A♯7 B♭7, B7, C7, C♯7 D♭7, D7, D♯7 E♭7, E7, F7, F♯7 G♭7, G7, G♯7 A♭7

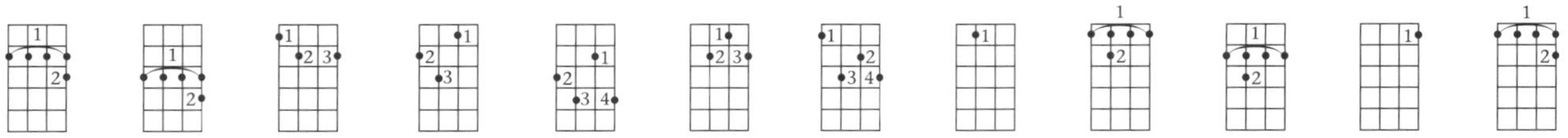

Minor Seventh Chords

Am7, A♯m7 B♭m7, Bm7, Cm7, C♯m7 D♭m7, Dm7, D♯m7 E♭m7, Em7, Fm7, F♯m7 G♭m7, Gm7, G♯m7 A♭m7

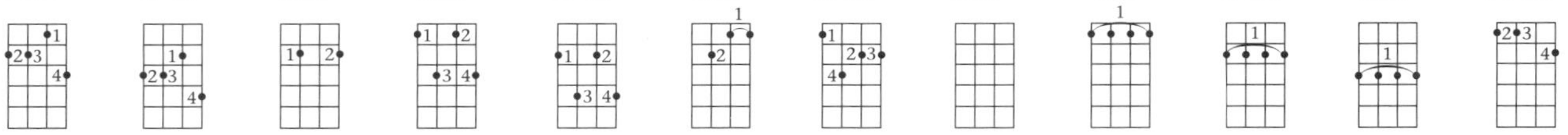

Major Sixth Chords

A6, A♯6 B♭6, B6, C6, C♯6 D♭6, D6, D♯6 E♭6, E6, F6, F♯6 G♭6, G6, G♯6 A♭6

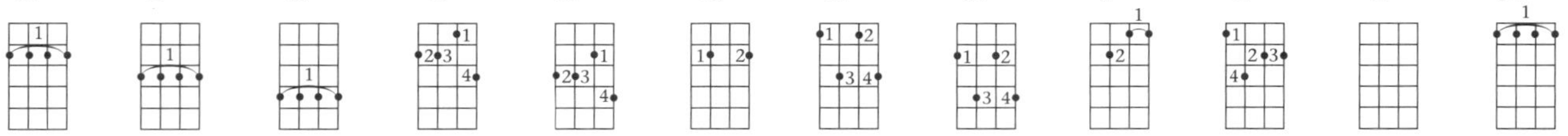

Minor Sixth Chords

Am6, A♯m6 B♭m6, Bm6, Cm6, C♯m6 D♭m6, Dm6, D♯m6 E♭m6, Em6, Fm6, F♯m6 G♭m6, Gm6, G♯m6 A♭m6

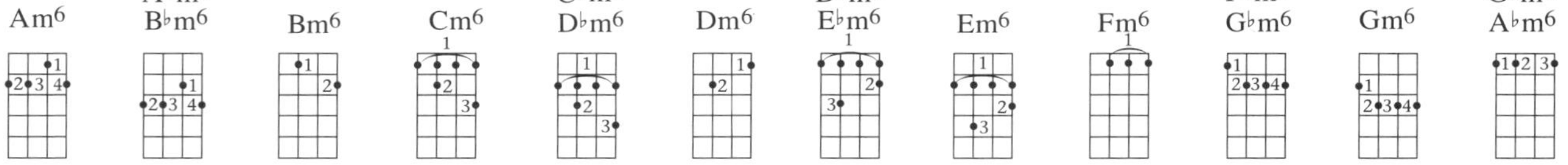

Major Seventh Chords

Amaj7, A♯maj7 B♭maj7, Bmaj7, Cmaj7, C♯maj7 D♭maj7, Dmaj7, D♯maj7 E♭maj7, Emaj7, Fmaj7, F♯maj7 G♭maj7, Gmaj7, G♯maj7 A♭maj7

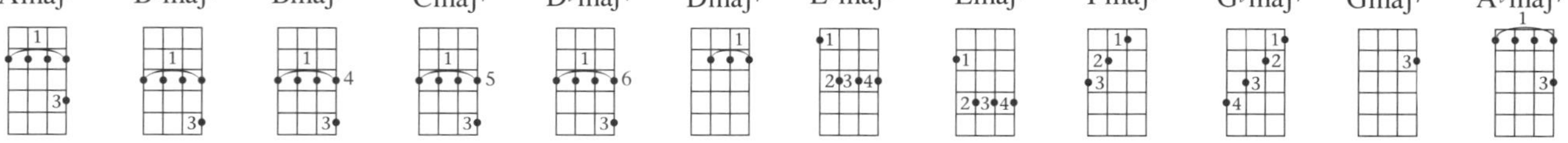

Augmented Fifth Chords (+ or aug)

A+, A♯+ B♭+, B+, C+, C♯+ D♭+, D+, D♯ E♭, E+, F+, F♯+ G♭+, G+, G♯+ A♭+

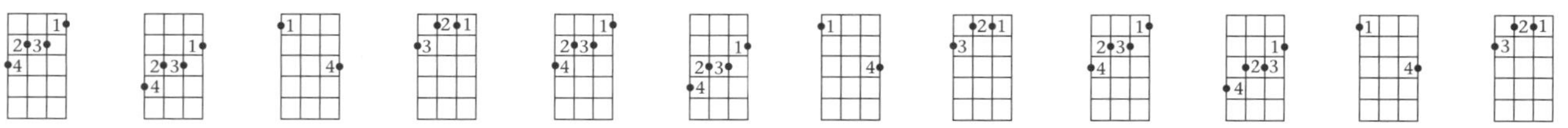

Diminished Seventh Chords (dim)

Adim, A♯dim B♭dim, Bdim, Cdim, C♯dim D♭dim, Ddim, D♯dim E♭dim, Edim, Fdim, F♯dim G♭dim, Gdim, G♯dim A♭dim

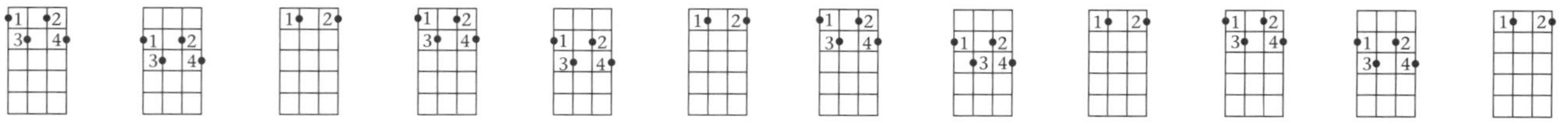

Are You Lonesome Tonight?

Words and Music by
ROY TURK and LOU HANDMAN

TRO - © Copyright 1926 (Renewed) Cromwell Music, Inc. and Bourne Co. (ASCAP), New York, NY

13

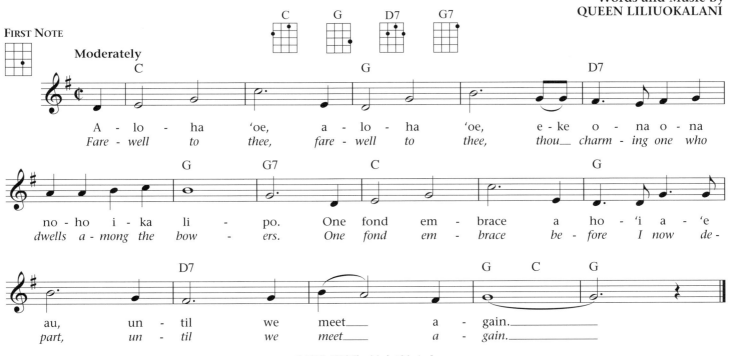

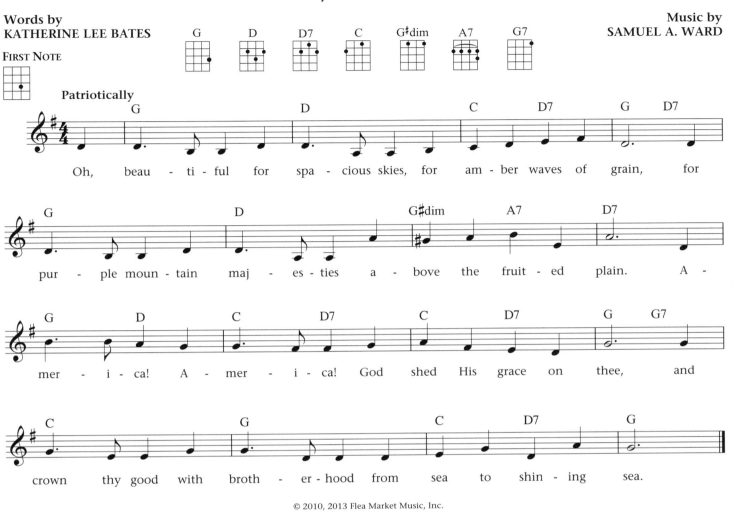

Anchors Aweigh

Words by ALFRED HART MILES
and ROYAL LOVELL
Additional Lyric by
GEORGE D. LOTTMAN

Music by
CHARLES A. ZIMMERMAN

First Note

Spirited March

Stand Na-vy out to sea, fight our bat-tle cry;___ we'll nev-er change our course, so vi-cious foe steer shy-y-y-y. Roll out the T. N. T. an-chors a-weigh.___ Sail on to vic-to-ry and sink their bones to Da-vy Jones hoo-ray!___

© 2010, 2013 Flea Market Music, Inc.

Baby, Won't You Please Come Home

Words and Music by CHARLES WARFIELD
and CLARENCE WILLIAMS

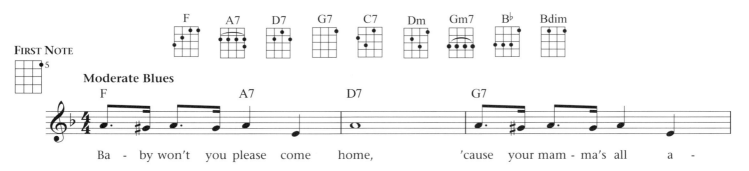

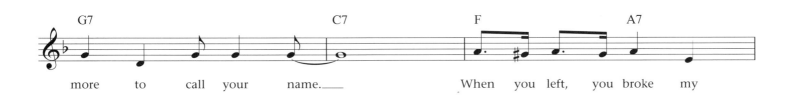

© 2010, 2013 Flea Market Music, Inc.

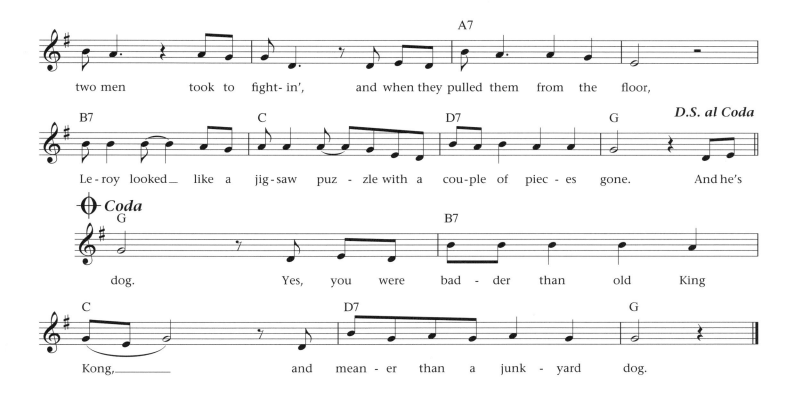

Baby Face

Words and Music by BENNY DAVIS and HARRY AKST

Copyright © 1926 (Renewed) B & G AKST PUBLISHING CO. and BENNY DAVIS MUSIC
All Rights for B & G AKST PUBLISHING CO. Administered by THE SONGWRITERS GUILD OF AMERICA
Harry Akst Reversionary Interest Controlled by BOURNE CO. (ASCAP)

Beautiful Brown Eyes

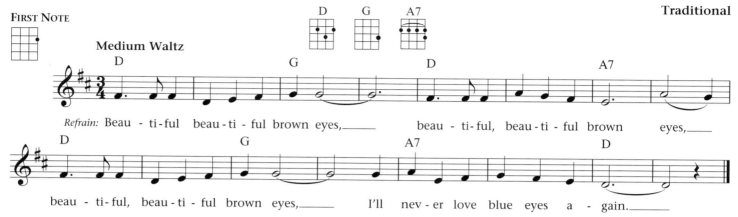

Traditional

Refrain: Beau-ti-ful beau-ti-ful brown eyes,_____ beau-ti-ful, beau-ti-ful brown eyes,_____ beau-ti-ful, beau-ti-ful brown eyes,_____ I'll nev-er love blue eyes a-gain._____

Additional Lyrics

1. Willie, my darling, I love you,
   love you with all of my heart.
   Tomorrow we might have been married,
   but drinkin' has kept us apart.
   Refrain

2. Seven long years I've been married.
   I wish I was single again.
   A woman never knows of her troubles
   until she has married a man.
   Refrain

3. Down to the barroom he staggered;
   staggered and fell at the door.
   The very last words he uttered:
   "I'll never get drunk any more."
   Refrain

© 2010, 2013 Flea Market Music, Inc.

The Best Things In Life Are Free

Words and Music by
B.G. DeSYLVA, LEW BROWN,
and RAY HENDERSON

The moon be-longs to ev-'ry-one,_____ the best things in life are free._____ The stars be-long to ev-'ry-one,_____ they gleam there for you and me._____ The flow-ers in spring,_____ the rob-ins that sing,— the sun-beams that shine,_____ they're yours, they're mine! And love can come to ev-'ry-one; the best things in life are free._____

Copyright © 1927 by Chappell & Co., Stephen Ballentine Music Publishing Co. and Ray Henderson Music Co.
Copyright Renewed

Blowin' In The Wind

Words and Music by BOB DYLAN

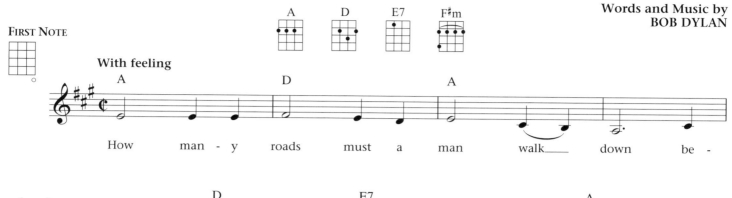
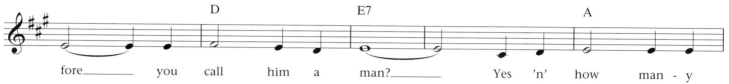

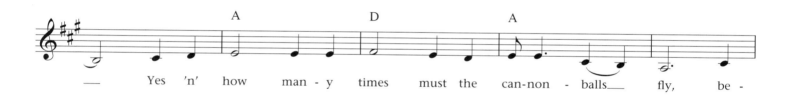

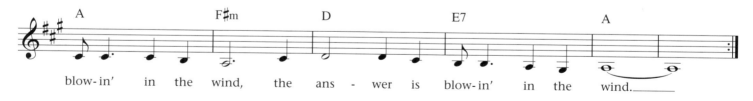

Additional Lyrics

2. How many times must a man look up, before he can see the sky?
   Yes 'n' how many ears must one man have, before he can hear people cry?
   Yes 'n' how many deaths will it take 'til he knows, that too many people have died?
   The answer my friend, is blowin' in the wind, the answer is blowin' in the wind.

3. How many years can a mountain exist, before it is washed to the sea?
   Yes 'n' how many years can some people exist, before they're allowed to be free?
   Yes 'n' how many times can a man turn his head, pretending that he just doesn't see?
   The answer my friend, is blowin' in the wind, the answer is blowin' in the wind.

Copyright © 1962 Warner Bros. Inc.
Copyright Renewed 1990 Special Rider Music

Blue Hawaii

Words and Music by LEO ROBIN and RALPH RAINGER

Blue Skies

© Copyright 1927 by Irving Berlin
Copyright Renewed

Bye Bye Blues

Copyright © 1930 by Bourne Co. (ASCAP)
Copyright Renewed

Additional Lyrics

2. Whatever happened to Tuesday and so slow
going down the old mine with a transistor radio.
Standing in the sunlight laughing,
hiding behind a rainbow's wall.
Slipping and a-sliding,
all along the waterfall
with you, my brown eyed girl,
you, my brown eyed girl.
Do you remember when we used to sing:
  Chorus

3. So hard to find my way, now that I'm all on my own.
I saw you just the other day, my, how you have grown.
Cast my memory back there, Lord;
sometime I'm overcome thinking 'bout
making love in the green grass
behind the stadium,
with you, my brown eyed girl,
with you, my brown eyed girl.
Do you remember when we used to sing:
  Chorus

Copyright © 1967 UNIVERSAL MUSIC PUBLISHING INTERNATIONAL LTD
Copyright Renewed
All Rights for the U.S. and Canada Controlled and Administered by UNIVERSAL - SONGS OF POLYGRAM INTERNATIONAL, INC.

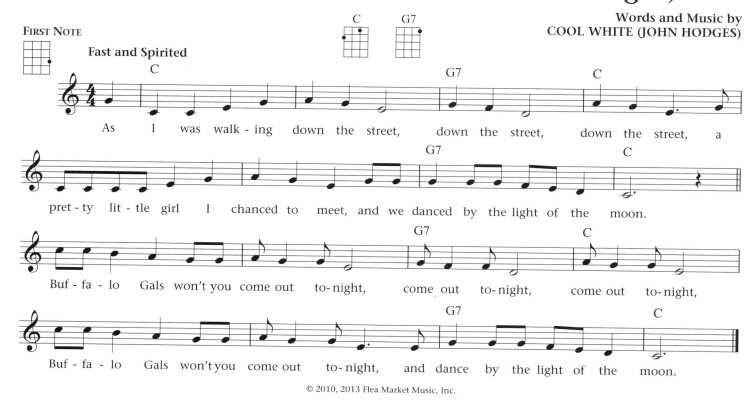

By The Beautiful Sea

Words by
HAROLD R. ATTERIDGE

Music by
HARRY CARROLL

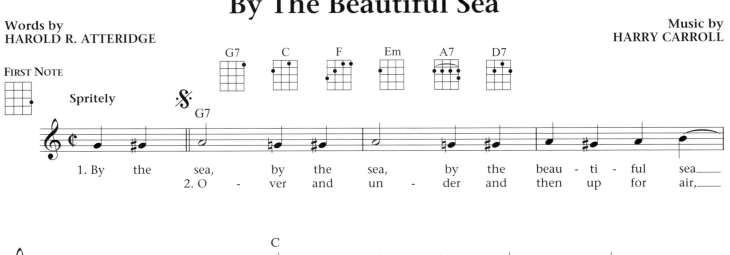

1. By the sea, by the sea, by the beau-ti-ful sea
2. O-ver and un-der and then up for air,

— you and I, you and I, oh how
— Pa is rich, Ma is rich, so now

To Coda

hap-py we'll be. When each wave comes a-
what do we care?

roll - ing in, we will duck or

D.S. al Coda

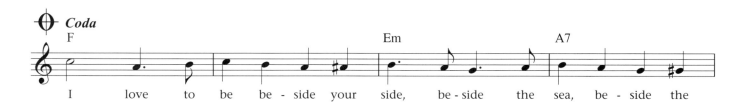

swim, and we'll float and fool a - round the wa-ter.

Coda

I love to be be-side your side, be-side the sea, be-side the sea - side, by the beau-ti-ful sea.

© 2010, 2013 Flea Market Music, Inc.

By The Light Of The Silvery Moon

Words by ED MADDE

Music by GUS EDWARDS

© 2010, 2013 Flea Market Music, Inc.

Come And Go With Me

Spiritual

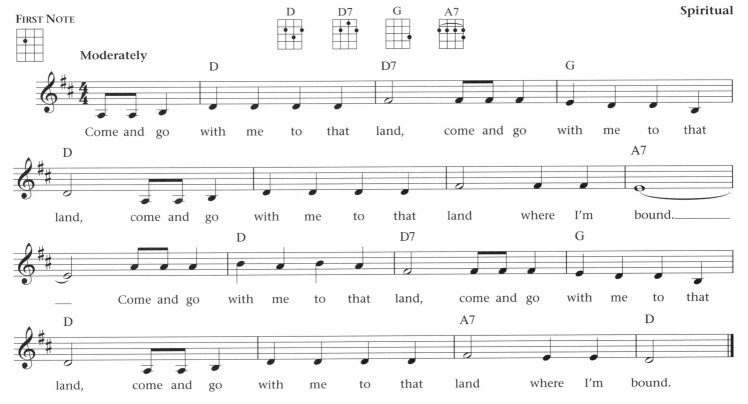

Additional Lyrics

2. There will be freedom in that land...
3. There will be singing in that land...
4. There will be peace in that land...
5. Come and go with me to that land...

© 2010, 2013 Flea Market Music, Inc.

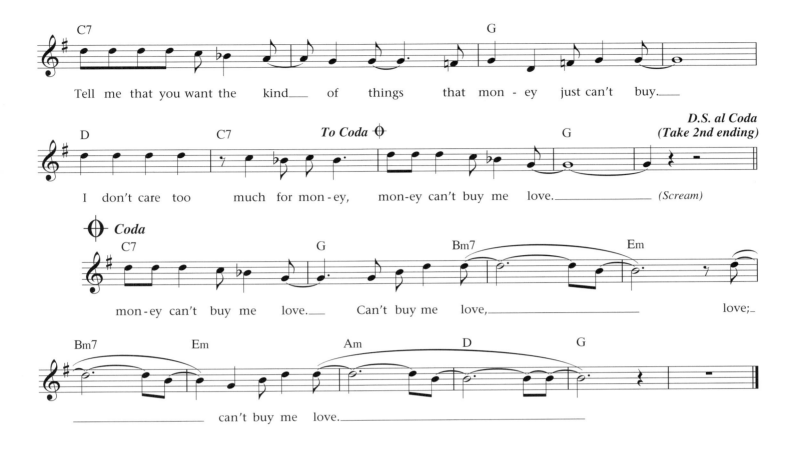

Careless Love

Traditional

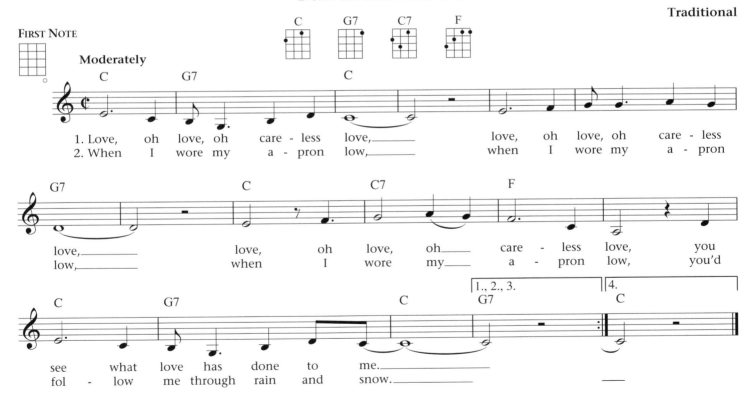

Additional Lyrics

3. Now my apron strings don't pin.
   Now my apron strings don't pin.
   Now my apron strings don't pin.
   You pass my door and you don't come in.

4. I cried last night and the night before.
   I cried last night and the night before.
   I cried last night and the night before.
   Gonna cry tonight and cry no more.

© 2010, 2013 Flea Market Music, Inc.

Can't Help Falling In Love

Words and Music by GEORGE DAVID WEISS, HUGO PERETTI and LUIGI CREATORE

Wise men say only fools rush in, but I can't help falling in love with you.
Shall I stay? Would it be a sin? If I can't help falling in love with you.

Like a river flows surely to the sea, darling so it goes, some things are meant to be. Take my hand, take my whole life too, for I can't help falling in love with you, for I can't help falling in love with you.

Copyright © 1961; Renewed 1989 Gladys Music (ASCAP)
Worldwide Rights for Gladys Music Administered by Cherry Lane Music Publishing Company, Inc.

Clementine

Words and Music by PERCY MONTROSE

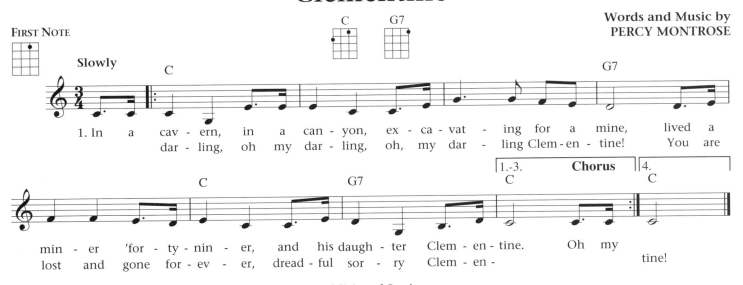

1. In a cavern, in a canyon, excavating for a mine, lived a miner 'forty-niner, and his daughter Clementine.

Oh my darling, oh my darling, oh, my darling Clementine! You are lost and gone forever, dreadful sorry Clementine.

Additional Lyrics

2. Light she was and, like a fairy,
   and her shoes were number nine;
   herring boxes, without topses,
   sandals were for Clementine.
   Chorus

3. Drove she ducklings to the water,
   every morning just at nine;
   hit her foot against a splinter,
   fell into the foaming brine.
   Chorus

4. Ruby lips above the water
   blowing bubbles soft and fine;
   but alas I was no swimmer,
   so I lost my Clementine.
   Chorus

© 2010, 2013 Flea Market Music, Inc.

51

Chicago
(That Toddlin' Town)

Words and Music by
FRED FISHER

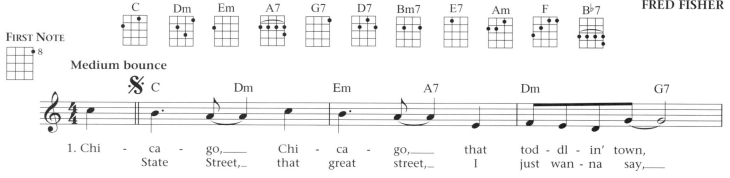

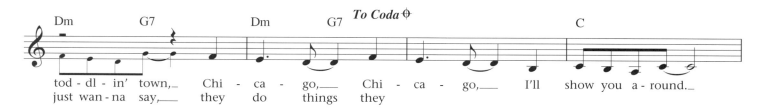

1. Chi - ca - go,___ Chi - ca - go,___ that tod - dl - in' town,
State Street,___ that great street,___ I just wan - na say,___

tod - dl - in' town,___ Chi - ca - go,___ Chi - ca - go,___ I'll show you a - round.___
just wan - na say,___ they do things they

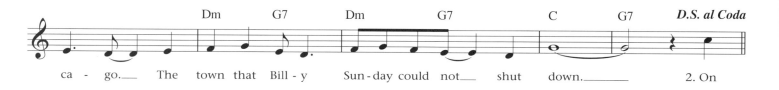

I love it! Bet your bot - tom dol - lar you'll lose the blues___ in Chi - ca - go,___ Chi -

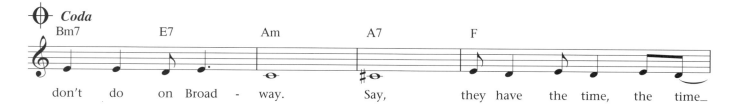

ca - go.___ The town that Bill - y Sun - day could not___ shut down.___ 2. On

don't do on Broad - way. Say, they have the time, the time___

___ of their life. I saw a man and he danced with his wife in Chi -

ca - go,___ Chi - ca - go, my home - town.___

© 2010, 2013 Flea Market Music, Inc.

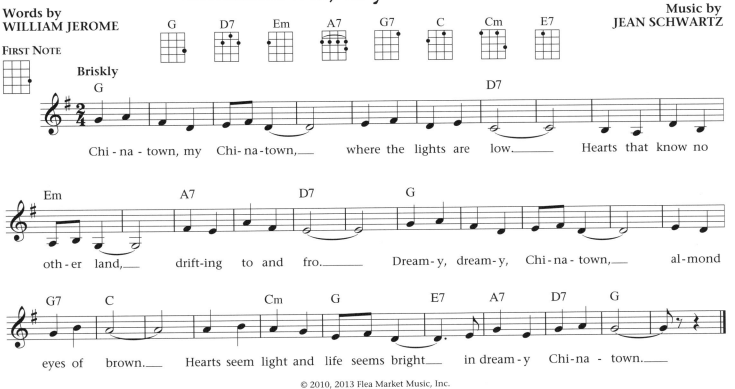

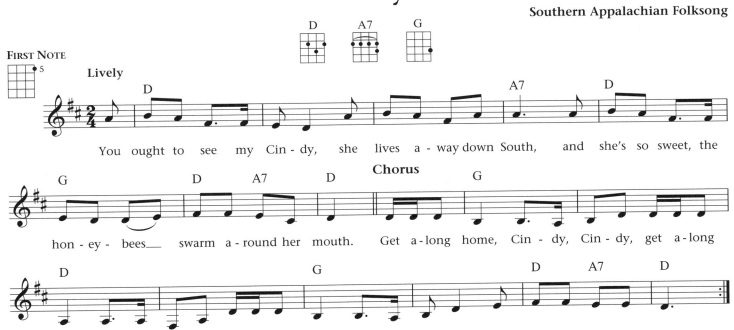

Additional Lyrics

2. I wish I was an apple,
   a-hangin' on the tree,
   and every time that Cindy passed,
   she'd take a bite of me.
   Chorus

3. I wish I had a needle,
   as fine as I could sew.
   I'd sew that gal to my coattail,
   and down the road we'd go.
   Chorus

4. Cindy in the springtime,
   Cindy in the fall,
   if I can't have my Cindy,
   I'll have no gal at all.
   Chorus

© 2010, 2013 Flea Market Music, Inc.

55

Crazy

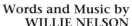

3. Whistle
   Whistle
   Whistle
   Whistle
   And you can be sure that if you're feelin' right,
   a daydream will last 'til long into the night.
   Tomorrow at breakfast you may pick up your ears,
   or you may be daydreamin' for a thousand years.

Dinah

Words by
SAM M. LEWIS and JOE YOUNG

Music by
HARRY AKST

© 1925 MILLS MUSIC, INC.
© Renewed MORLEY MUSIC CO., B & G AKST PUBLISHING CO. and MILLS MUSIC, INC.
Harry Akst Reversionary Interest Controlled by BOURNE CO. (ASCAP)

Down By The Riverside

Additional Lyrics

2. I'm gonna join hands with everyone,
   down by the riverside, down by the riverside,
   down by the riverside.
   I'm gonna join hands with everyone,
   down by the riverside,
   and study war no more.
   Chorus

© 2010, 2013 Flea Market Music, Inc.

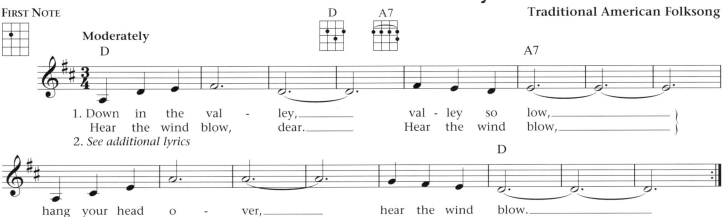

Additional Lyrics

2. Roses love sunshine, violets love dew;
   angels in heaven, know I love you.
   Know I love you dear, know I love you.
   angels in heaven know I love you.

3. Build me a castle forty feet high,
   so I can see him as he rides by.
   As he rides by love, as he rides by.
   So I can see him as he rides by.

4. If you don't love me, love whom you please,
   throw your arms 'round me, give my heart ease.
   Give my heart ease, love, give my heart ease.
   Throw your arms 'round me, give my heart ease.

5. Write me a letter, send it by mail.
   Send it in care of Birmingham jail.
   Birmingham jail, love, Birmingham jail.
   Send it in care of Birmingham jail.

© 2010, 2013 Flea Market Music, Inc.

TRO - © Copyright 1930 (Renewed) and 1931 (Renewed) Essex Music, Inc.,
Words and Music, Inc., New York, NY, Don Swan Publications, Miami, FL and Gilbert Keyes Music, Hollywood, CA

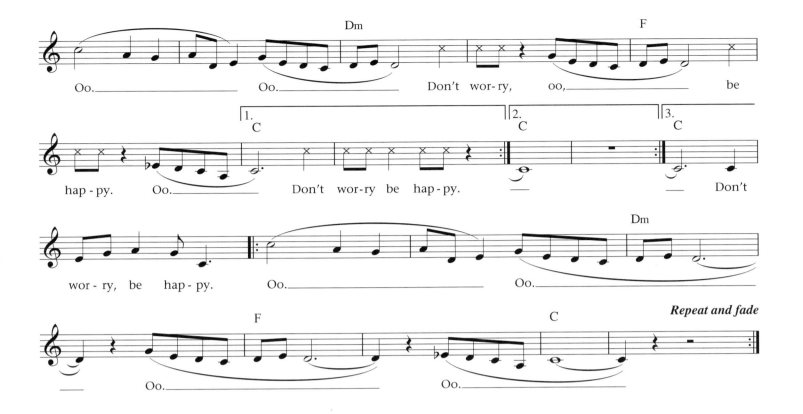

The Drunken Sailor

Sea Chanty

Additional Lyrics

3. Give 'im a dose of salt and water,
   give 'im a dose of salt and water,
   give 'im a dose of salt and water
   earlye in the morning.
   Chorus

4. Shave his belly with a rusty razor,
   shave his belly with a rusty razor,
   shave his belly with a rusty razor
   earlye in the morning.
   Chorus

© 2010, 2013 Flea Market Music, Inc.

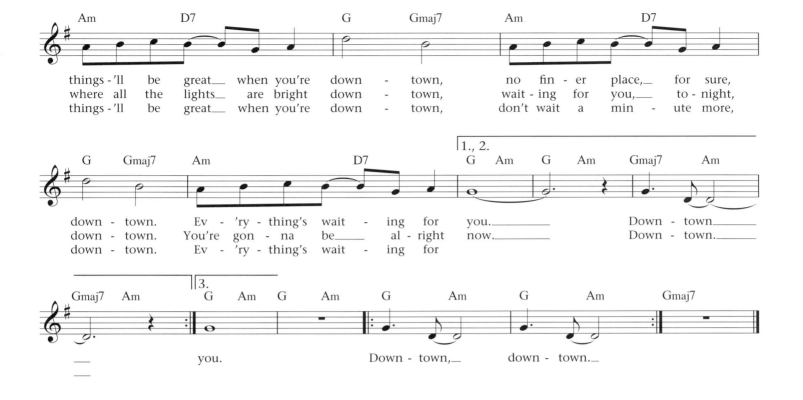

Ev'ry Time I Feel The Spirit

African-American Spiritual

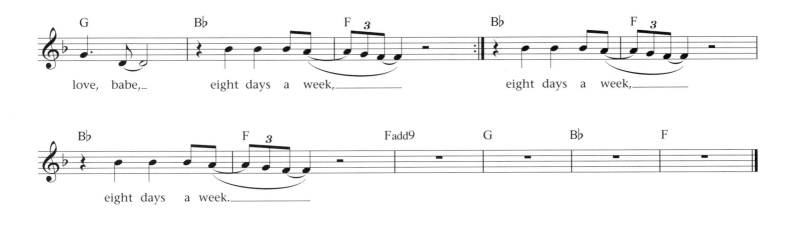

Edelweiss

Words by OSCAR HAMMERSTEIN II
Music by RICHARD RODGERS

Enjoy Yourself
(It's Later Than You Think)

Words by
HERB MAGIDSON

Music by
CARL SIGMAN

1. You work and work for years and years, you're always on the go. You never take a minute off, too busy making dough. Some day, you say, you'll have your fun when you're a millionaire. Imagine all the fun you'll have in your old rockin' chair.

2. You're gonna take that ocean trip, no matter come what may. You've got your reservations, but you just can't get away. Next year, for sure, you'll see the world, you'll really get around. But how far can you travel when you're six feet under ground?

Enjoy yourself, it's later than you think. Enjoy yourself, while you're still in the pink. The years go by as quickly as a wink. Enjoy yourself, enjoy yourself, it's later than you think.

Copyright © 1948 (Renewed) Music Sales Corporation and Magidson Music Co., Inc.

The Erie Canal

Traditional

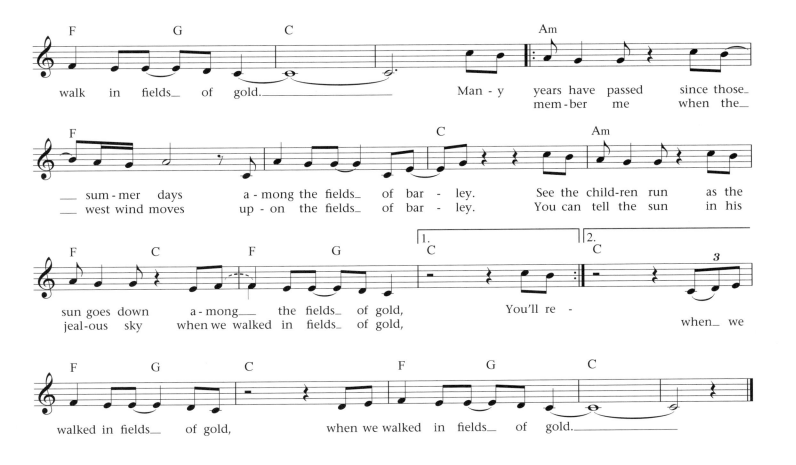

For He's A Jolly Good Fellow

Traditional

© 2010, 2013 Flea Market Music, Inc.

81

Folsom Prison Blues

Words and Music by
JOHN R. CASH

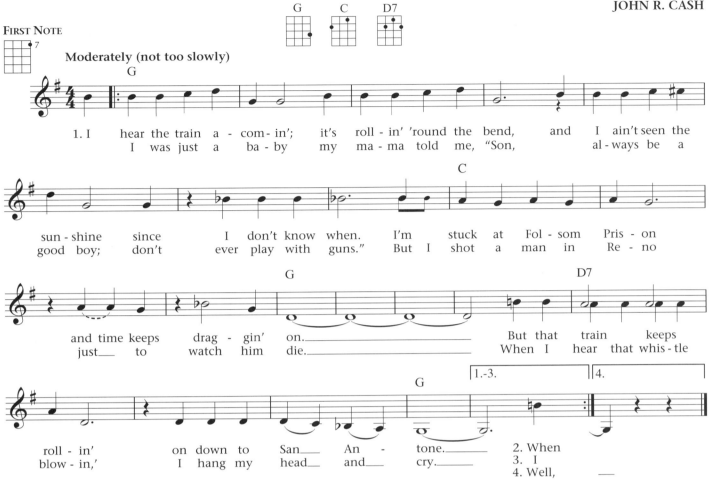

Additional Lyrics

3. I bet there's rich folks eatin' in a fancy dining car.
   They're prob'ly drinkin' coffee and smokin' big cigars.
   But I know I had it comin', I know I can't be free.
   But those people keep a-movin', and that's what tortures me.

4. Well, if they freed me from this prison, if that railroad train was mine,
   I bet I'd move on over a little farther down the line.
   Far from Folsom Prison, that's where I want to stay,
   and I'd let that lonesome whistle blow my blues away.

© 1956 (Renewed 1984) HOUSE OF CASH, INC. (BMI)/Administered by BUG MUSIC

From Me To You

Words and Music by JOHN LENNON
and PAUL McCARTNEY

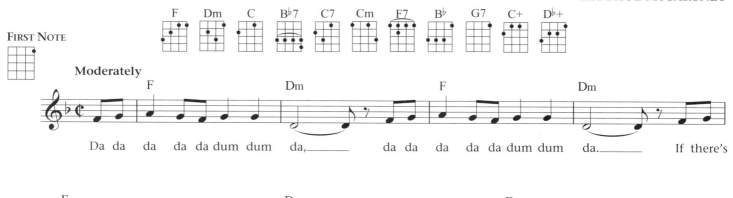

Da da da da da dum dum da,_____ da da da da da dum dum da._____ If there's

an-y-thing that you want,_____ if there's an-y-thing I can do,_____
ev-'ry-thing that you want,_____ like a heart_ that's oh so true,_

just call on me_ and I'll send it a-long,_ with love_ from me_ to you._

I got   I got arms that long to hold_ you, and

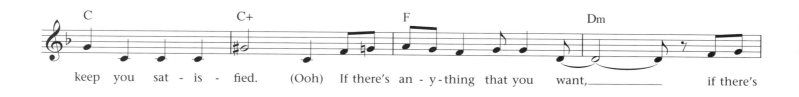

keep you by my_ side._____ I got lips that long to kiss_ you, and

keep you sat-is-fied. (Ooh) If there's an-y-thing that you want,_____ if there's

an-y-thing I can do,_____ just call on me_ and I'll

Copyright © 1963 by NORTHERN SONGS LTD., London, England
Copyright Renewed
All rights for the U.S.A., its territories and possessions and Canada
assigned to and controlled by GIL MUSIC CORP., 1650 Broadway, New York, NY 10019

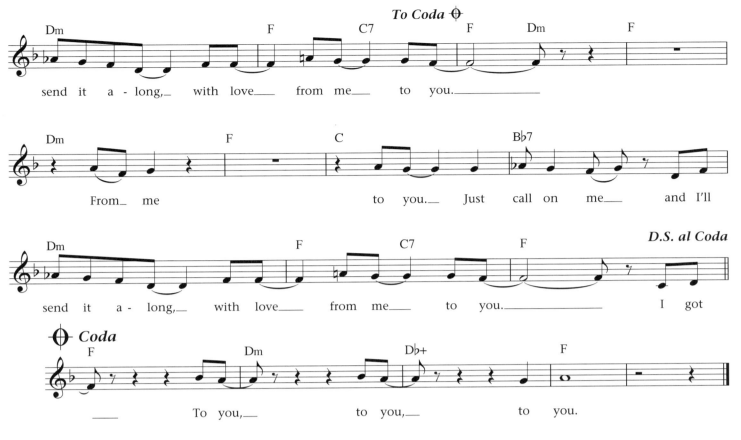

Georgia On My Mind

Words by STUART GORRELL
Music by HOAGY CARMICHAEL

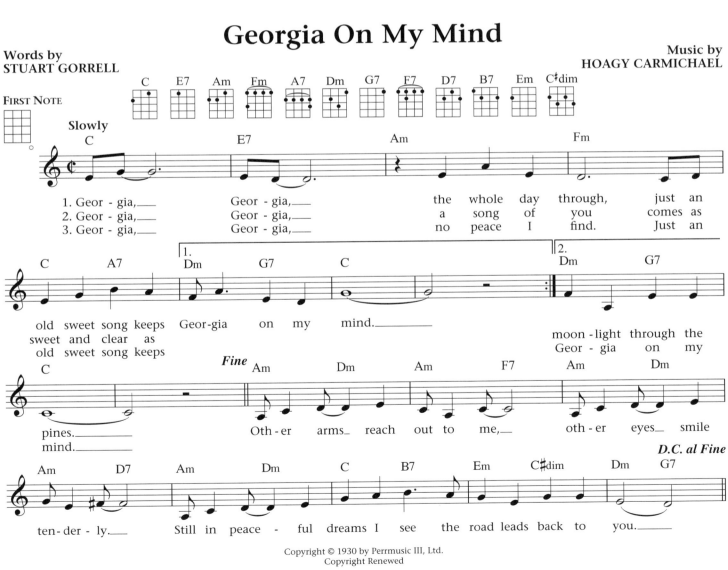

Give My Regards To Broadway

Words and Music by GEORGE M. COHAN

© 2010, 2013 Flea Market Music, Inc.

Give Me That Old Time Religion

Additional Lyrics

2. It was good for the Hebrew children,
it was good for the Hebrew children,
it was good for the Hebrew children,
it's good enough for me.

3. It was good for our mothers,
it was good for our mothers,
it was good for our mothers,
it's good enough for me.

4. It will take us all to heaven,
it will take us all to heaven,
it will take us all to heaven,
it's good enough for me.

© 2010, 2013 Flea Market Music, Inc.

The Glory Of Love

Copyright © 1936 Shapiro, Bernstein & Co., Inc., New York
Copyright Renewed

Go Down, Moses

Traditional American Spiritual

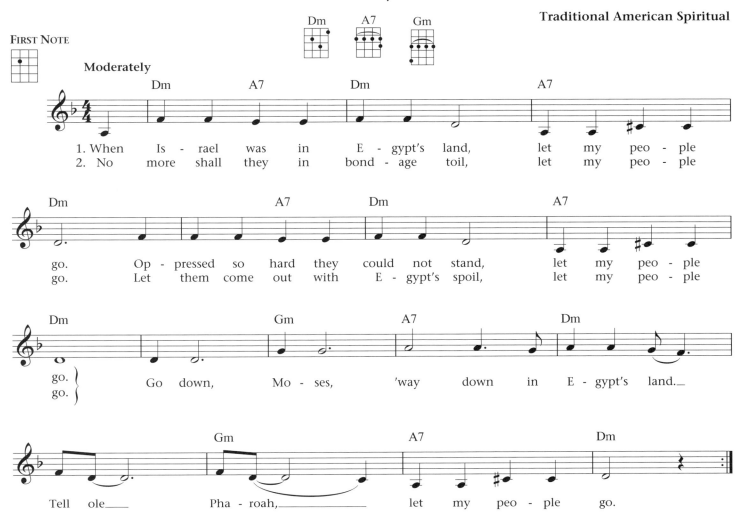

Additional Lyrics

The Lord told Moses what to do, let my people go.
To lead the Hebrew children through, let my people go.
Chorus

O come along Moses, you'll not get lost, let my people go.
Stretch out your rod and come across, let my people go.
Chorus

As Israel stood by the waterside, let my people go.
At God's command it did divide, let my people go.
Chorus

When they reached the other shore, let my people go.
They sang a song of triumph o'er, let my people go.
Chorus

Pharaoh said he'd go across, let my people go.
But Pharaoh and his host were lost, let my people go.
Chorus

Jordan shall stand up like a wall, let my people go.
And the walls of Jericho shall fall, let my people go.
Chorus

Your foes shall not before you stand, let my people go.
And you'll possess fair Canaan's Land, let my people go.
Chorus

We need not always weep and mourn, let my people go.
And wear these slavery chains forlorn, let my people go.
Chorus

© 2010, 2013 Flea Market Music, Inc.

Goodnight, Irene

Words and Music by
HUDDIE LEDBETTER
and JOHN A. LOMAX

1. Last Saturday night I got married, me and my wife settled down. Now me and my wife are parted, I'm gonna take another walk downtown.
2. Sometimes I live in the country, sometimes I live in the town. Sometimes I have a great notion to jump into the river and drown.
3. Stop ramblin', stop your gamblin', stop staying out late at night. Go home to your wife and your fam'ly, sit down by the fireside bright.

TRO - © Copyright 1936 (Renewed) and 1950 (Renewed) Ludlow Music, Inc., New York, NY

A Groovy Kind Of Love

Hawaii Ponoi
(Hawaiian National Anthem)

Words and Music by
KING KALAKAUA
and HENRI BERGER

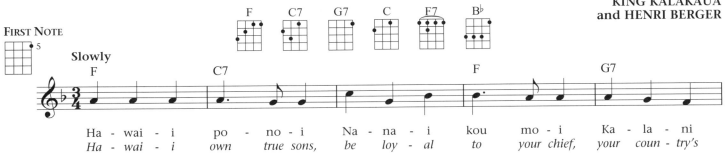

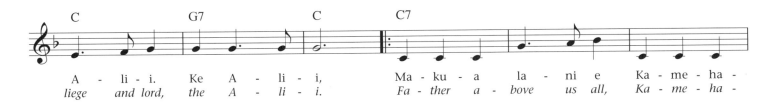

Ha - wai - i po - no - i, Na - na i kou mo - i Ka - la - ni
Ha - wai - i own true sons, be loy - al to your chief, your coun - try's

A - li - i. Ke A - li - i, Ma - ku - a la - ni e Ka - me - ha -
liege and lord, the A - li - i. Fa - ther a - bove us all, Ka - me - ha -

me - ha e Na ka - ua e pa - le Me ka i - he.
me - ha e, who guard - ed in the war with his i - he.

© 2010, 2013 Flea Market Music, Inc.

He's Got The Whole World In His Hands

Traditional Spiritual

Additional Lyrics

2. He's got the little bitty baby in His hands…
3. He's got you and me, sister, in His hands…
4. He's got you and me, brother, in His hands…
5. He's got a little ukulele in His hands…
6. He's got the whole world in His hands…

© 2010, 2013 Flea Market Music, Inc

Home On The Range

Words by
DR. BREWSTER HIGLEY

Music by
DAN KELLY

Additional Lyrics

2. Oh, give me a land where the bright diamond sand
flows leisurely down the clear stream;
where the graceful white swan goes gliding along
like a maid in a heavenly dream.
   Chorus

3. How often at night, when the heavens are bright
with the light from the glittering stars,
have I stood there amazed and asked as I gazed
if their glory exceeds that of ours.
   Chorus

4. Where the air is so pure, and the zephyrs so free,
and the breezes so balmy and light,
that I would not exchange my home on the range
for all of the cities so bright.
   Chorus

© 2010. 2013 Flea Market Music, Inc.

How Can I Keep From Singing?

Words and Music by
ROBERT LOWRY

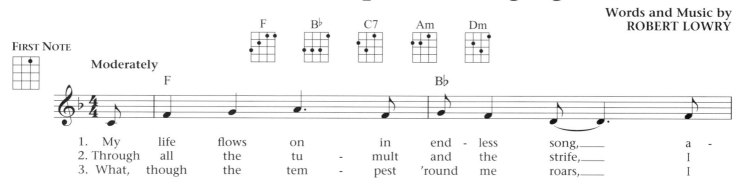

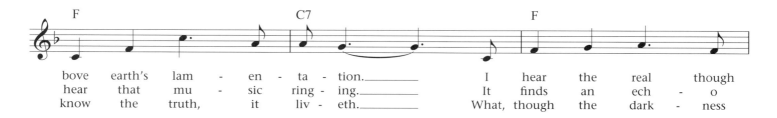

1. My life flows on in end - less song,___ a -
2. Through all the tu - mult and the strife,___ I
3. What, though the tem - pest 'round me roars,___ I

bove earth's lam - en - ta - tion.___ I hear the real though
hear that mu - sic ring - ing.___ It finds an ech - o
know the truth, it liv - eth.___ What, though the dark - ness

far - off hymn___ that hails a new cre - a - tion.___
in my soul;___ how can I keep from sing - ing?___ } No
gath - ers near,___ songs in the night it giv - eth.___

storm can shake my in - most calm,___ while to that rock I'm

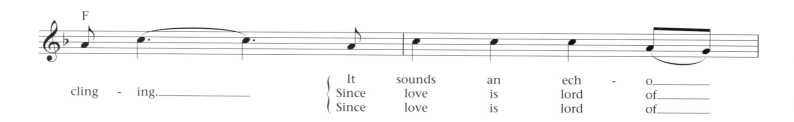

cling - ing.___
{ It sounds an ech - o
{ Since love is lord of___
{ Since love is lord of___

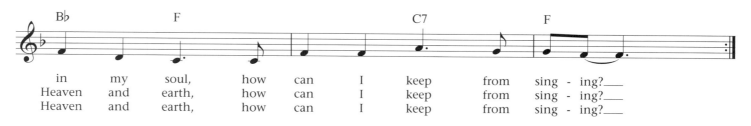

in my soul, how can I keep from sing - ing?___
Heaven and earth, how can I keep from sing - ing?___
Heaven and earth, how can I keep from sing - ing?___

© 2010, 2013 Flea Market Music, Inc.

How Sweet It Is
(To Be Loved By You)

Words and Music by
EDWARD HOLLAND, LAMONT DOZIER,
and BRIAN HOLLAND

With a beat

How sweet it is___ to be loved by you.

I need-ed the shel-ter of some-one's arms;___ there you
I close my eyes at___ night
(Instrumental)
were. I need-ed some-one to un-der-stand my ups and downs;___
you in my life.___ Ev-'ry-thing I did was just a bore;___
there you were___ ev-'ry-where I went, seems I'd been there be-fore.
(End Instrumental)
with sweet love and de-
You were bet-ter to me than I
vo-tion, deep-ly touch-ing my e-mo-tion.___
all of my days___ with a love so sweet in so man-y ways.___ I want to
was to my-self;___ for me there's___ you and there ain't no-bod-y else.___
stop and thank you, ba-by; I want___ to stop and thank you, ba-by.

How sweet it is___ to be loved by you. How sweet it is___ to be loved by
you. How sweet it is___ to be loved by you.

Repeat and Fade

© 1964 (Renewed 1992) JOBETE MUSIC CO., INC.
All Rights Controlled and Administered by EMI BLACKWOOD MUSIC INC. on behalf of STONE AGATE MUSIC (A Division of JOBETE MUSIC CO., INC.)

The Hukilau Song

I Ain't Got Nobody
(And Nobody Cares For Me)

Words by ROGER GRAHAM
Music by SPENCER WILLIAMS and DAVE PEYTON

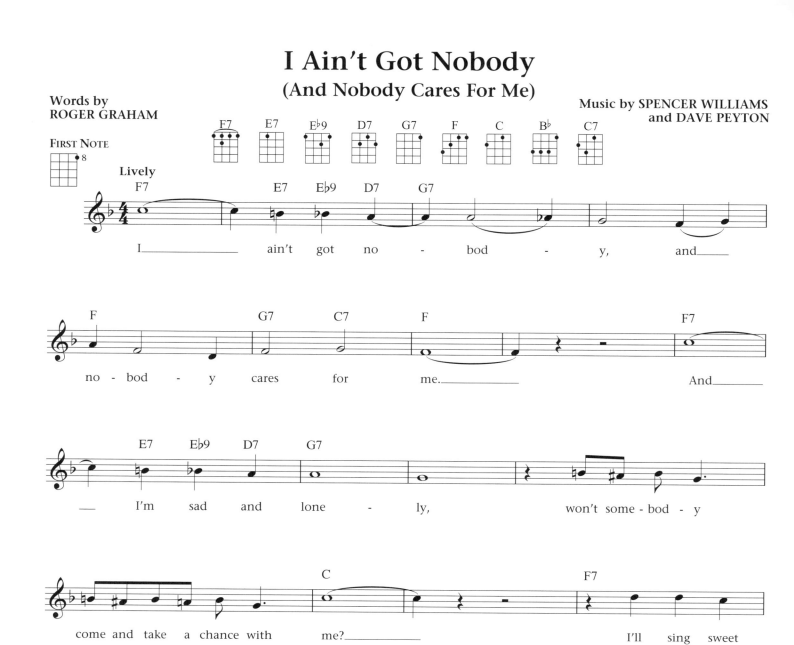

© 2010, 2013 Flea Market Music, Inc.

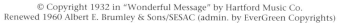

Indiana

Words by
BALLARD MacDONALD

Music by
JAMES F. HANLEY

Back home a-gain___ in In-di-an-a, and it seems that I can see___ the gleam-ing can-dle-light still shin-ing bright through the syc-a-mores for me.___ The new-mown hay___ sends all its fra-grance from the fields I used to roam.___ When I dream a-bout the moon-light on the Wa-bash, then I long for my In-di-an-a home.

© 2010, 2013 Flea Market Music, Inc.

129

In The Good Old Summertime

Words by
REN SHIELDS

Music by
GEORGE EVANS

I've Been Working On The Railroad

American Folksong

134

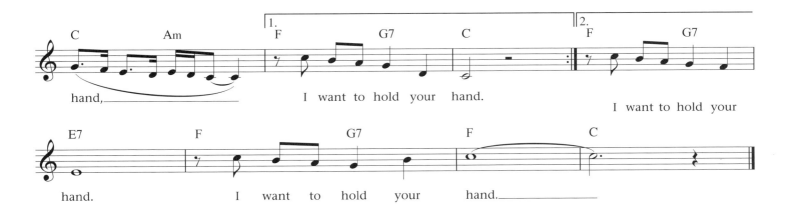

It's My Party

Words and Music by HERB WIENER, WALLY GOLD, and JOHN GLUCK, JR.

Copyright © 1963 by World Song Publishing, Inc.
Copyright Renewed
All Rights Administered by Chappell & Co.

I Walk The Line

Words and Music by JOHNNY CASH

Additional Lyrics

3. As sure as night is dark and day is light,
   I keep you on my mind both day and night.
   And happiness I've known proves that it's right.
   Because you're mine, I walk the line.

4. You've got a way to keep me on your side.
   You give me cause for love that I can't hide.
   For you I know I'd even try to turn the tide.
   Because you're mine, I walk the line.

5. I keep a close watch on this heart of mine.
   I keep my eyes wide open all the time.
   I keep the ends out for the tie that binds.
   Because you're mine, I walk the line.

© 1956 (Renewed 1984) HOUSE OF CASH, INC. (BMI)/Administered by BUG MUSIC

Ja-Da

Words and Music by BOB CARLETON

© 2010, 2013 Flea Market Music, Inc.

Jambalaya
(On The Bayou)

Words and Music by
HANK WILLIAMS

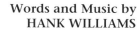

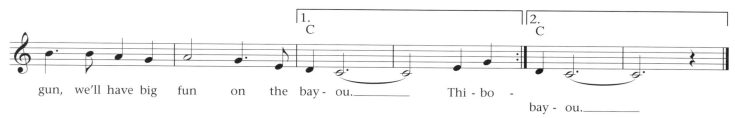

Good-bye, Joe, me got-ta go, me oh my oh. Me got-ta go pole the
daux, Fon-tain-eaux, the place is buzz-in'. Kin folk come to see Y-
pi-rogue down the bay-ou. My Yvonne, the sweet-est one, me oh my oh.
vonne by the doz-en. Dress in style and go hog wild, me oh my oh.
Son-of-a-gun, we'll have big fun on the bay-ou.
Son-of-a-gun, we'll have big fun on the bay-ou. Jam-ba-
la-ya and a craw-fish pie and fil-let gum-bo. 'Cause to-night I'm gon-na see my ma cher a
mi-o. Pick gui-tar, fill fruit jar and be gay-o. Son-of-a-
gun, we'll have big fun on the bay-ou. Thi-bo-
bay-ou.

Copyright © 1952 Sony/ATV Music Publishing LLC and Hiriam Music in the U.S.A.
Copyright Renewed
All Rights on behalf of Hiriam Music Administered by Rightsong Music Inc.
All Rights outside the U.S.A. Administered by Sony/ATV Music Publishing LLC
All Rights on behalf of Sony/ATV Music Publishing LLC Administered by Sony/ATV Music Publishing LLC, 8 Music Square West, Nashville, TN 37203

Keep On The Sunny Side

Kumbaya

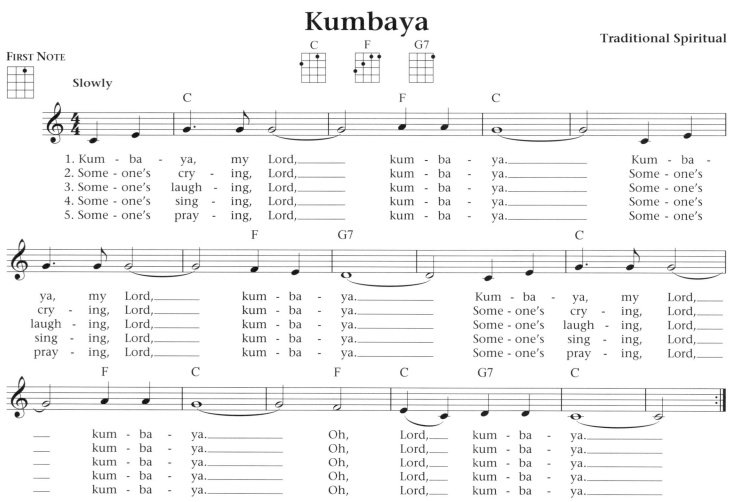

Last Train To Clarksville

Let It Be

Words and Music by
JOHN LENNON and PAUL McCARTNEY

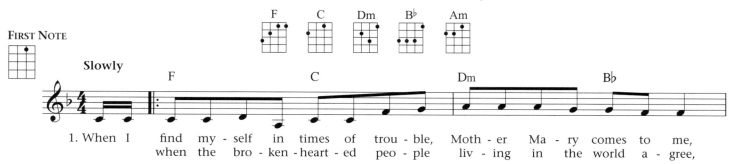

1. When I find my-self in times of trou-ble, Moth-er Ma-ry comes to me,
when the bro-ken-heart-ed peo-ple liv-ing in the world a-gree,

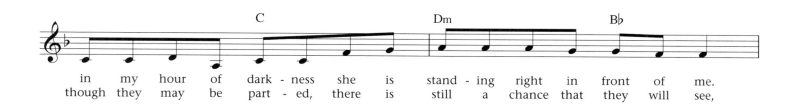

speak-ing words of wis-dom, let it be. And
there will be an an-swer, let it be. For

in my hour of dark-ness she is stand-ing right in front of me.
though they may be part-ed, there is still a chance that they will see,

Speak-ing words of wis-dom, let it be. Let it
there will be an an-swer, let it be.

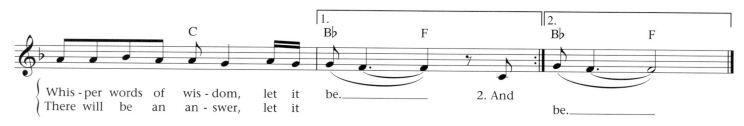

be, let it be, let it be, let it be.

Whis-per words of wis-dom, let it be. 2. And
There will be an an-swer, let it be.

Copyright © 1970 Sony/ATV Music Publishing LLC
Copyright Renewed
All Rights Administered by Sony/ATV Music Publishing LLC, 8 Music Square West, Nashville, TN 37203

The Letter

Words and Music by WAYNE CARSON THOMPSON

1.,3. Give me a tick-et for an air-plane, ain't got time to take the fast-est train.
2. I don't care how much mon-ey I got-ta spend, got to get back to my ba-by.

Lone-ly days are gone, I'm a-go-in' home, my ba-by just wrote me a let-ter. let-ter.

Well, she wrote me a let-ter, said she could-n't live with-out me no more. Lis-ten, mis-ter, can't you see I got to get back to my ba-by once more. An-y way.

Coda
let-ter. My ba-by just wrote me a let-ter. My

© 1967 (Renewed) Budde Songs, Inc.

Long, Long Ago

Words and Music by
THOMAS BAYLY

Tell me the tales that to me were so dear, long, long a-go,
Do you re-mem-ber the path where we met, long, long a-go,
Tho' by your kind-ness my fond hopes were raised, long, long a-go,

long, long a-go. Sing me the songs I de-light-ed to hear,
long, long a-go? Ah yes, you told me you ne'er would for-get,
long, long a-go, you, by more el-o-quent lips, have been praised,

long, long a-go, long a-go. Now you are come, all my grief is re-moved;
long, long a-go, long a-go. Then to all oth-ers, my smile you pre-ferred;
long, long a-go, long a-go. But by long ab-sence your truth has been tried;

let me for-get that so long you have roved. Let me be-lieve that you
love, when you spoke, gave a charm to each word. Still my heart treas-ures the
still, to your ac-cents, I lis-ten with pride. Blest as I was when I

love as you loved, long, long a-go, long a-go.
prais-es I heard, long, long a-go, long a-go.
sat by your side, long, long a-go, long a-go.

© 2010, 2013 Flea Market Music, Inc.

152

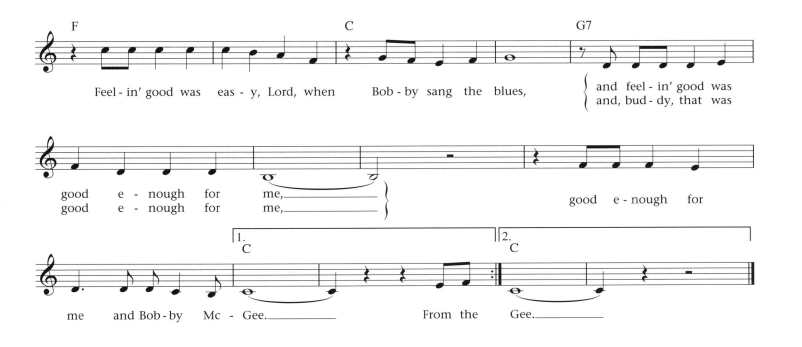

The Marine's Hymn

Words by
HENRY C. DAVIS

Melody based on a theme by
JACQUES OFFENBACH

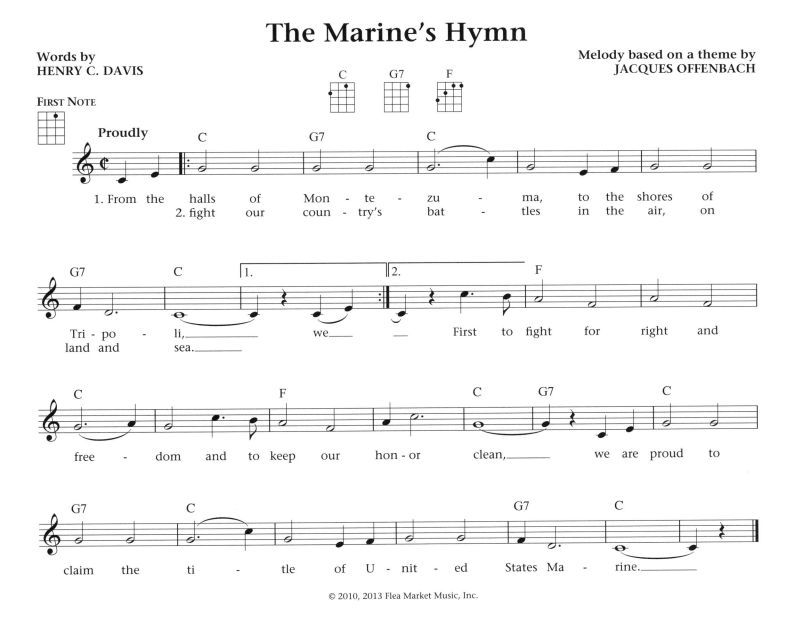

© 2010, 2013 Flea Market Music, Inc.

Midnight Special

Railroad Song

Additional Lyrics

2. Yonder comes Miss Rosie. How in the world did you know?
   By the way she wears her apron, and the clothes she wore.
   Umbrella on her shoulder, piece of paper in her hand.
   She come to tell the governor, "Turn loose of my man."
   Chorus

3. If you're ever in Houston, well you'd better walk right.
   You'd better not swagger, and you better not fight,
   or the sheriff will arrest you, he's gonna take you down.
   You can bet your bottom dollar, you're penitentiary bound.
   Chorus

© 2010, 2013 Flea Market Music, Inc.

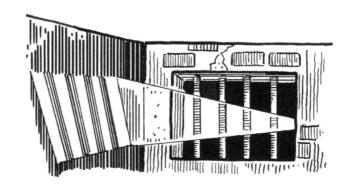

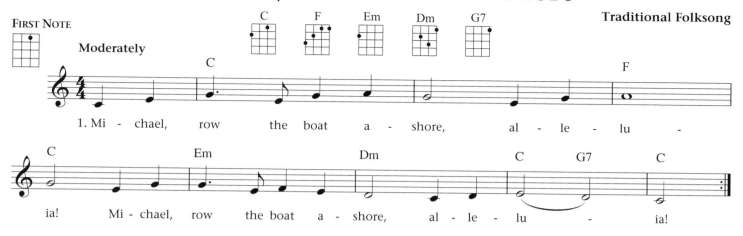

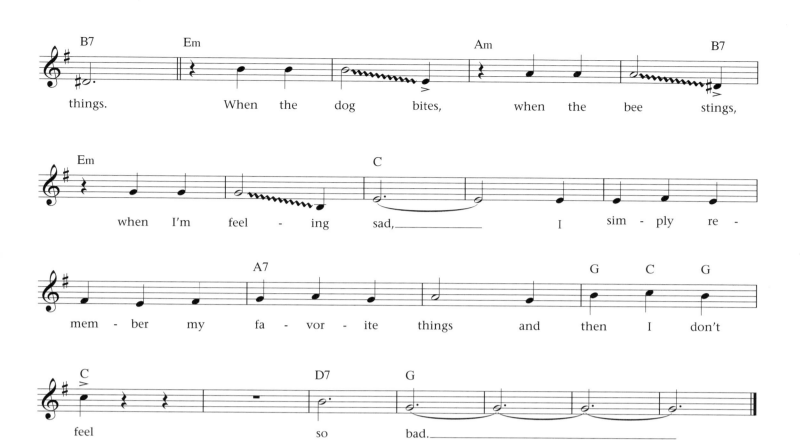

Moonlight Bay

Words by EDWARD MADDEN
Music by PERCY WENRICH

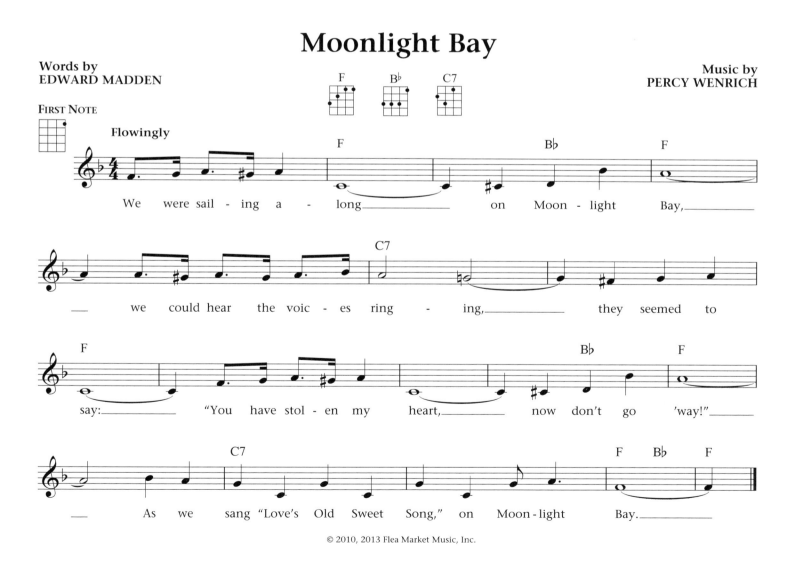

© 2010, 2013 Flea Market Music, Inc.

My Bonnie
(Lies Over The Ocean)

Traditional Scottish Song

My Blue Heaven

Words by GEORGE WHITING
Music by WALTER DONALDSON

Copyright © 1927 (Renewed) by Donaldson Publishing Co. and George Whiting Publishing

Nobody Knows The Trouble I've Seen

African-American Spiritual

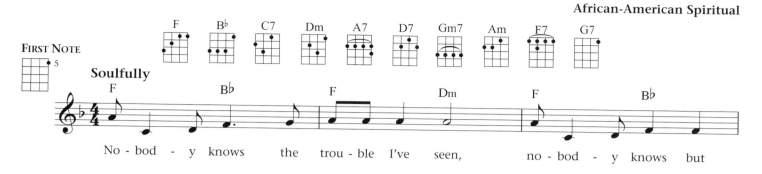

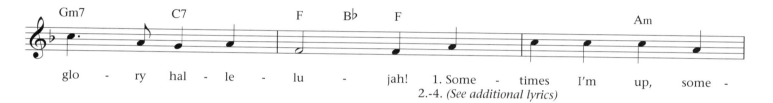

Additional Lyrics

2. Now you may think that I don't know,
   oh, yes, Lord!
   But I've had troubles here below,
   oh, yes, Lord!

3. One day when I was walkin' along,
   oh, yes, Lord!
   the sky opened up and love came down,
   oh, yes, Lord!

4. I never shall forget that day,
   oh, yes, Lord!
   when Jesus washed my sins away,
   oh, yes, Lord!

© 2010, 2013 Flea Market Music, Inc.

Oh, Susanna

Words and Music by STEPHEN FOSTER

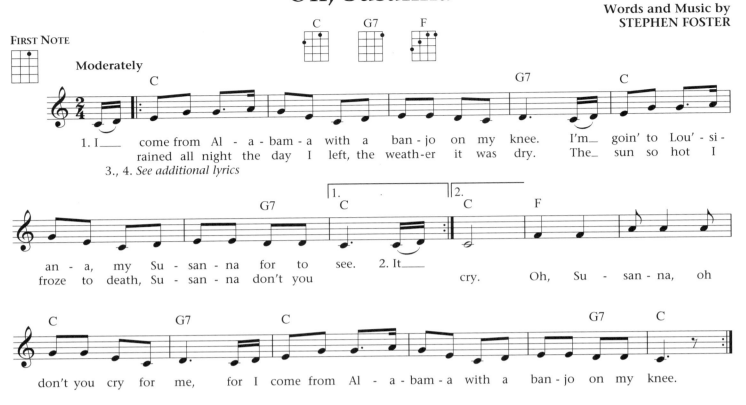

Additional Lyrics

3. I had a dream the other night, when everything was still;
   I thought I saw Susanna a-coming down the hill.

4. The buckwheat cake was in her mouth, the tear was in her eye.
   Says I, "I'm coming from the South; Susanna, don't you cry!"

© 2010, 2013 Flea Market Music, Inc.

On A Slow Boat To China

Words and Music by
FRANK LOESSER

© 1948 (Renewed) FRANK MUSIC CORP.

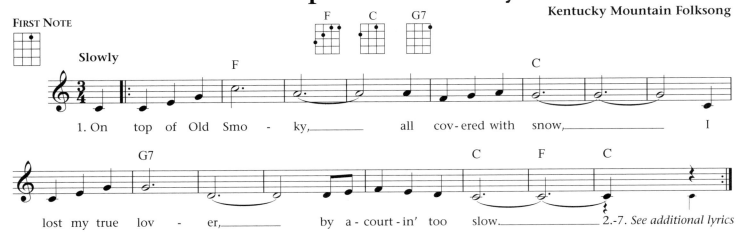

Peace Like A River

Spiritual

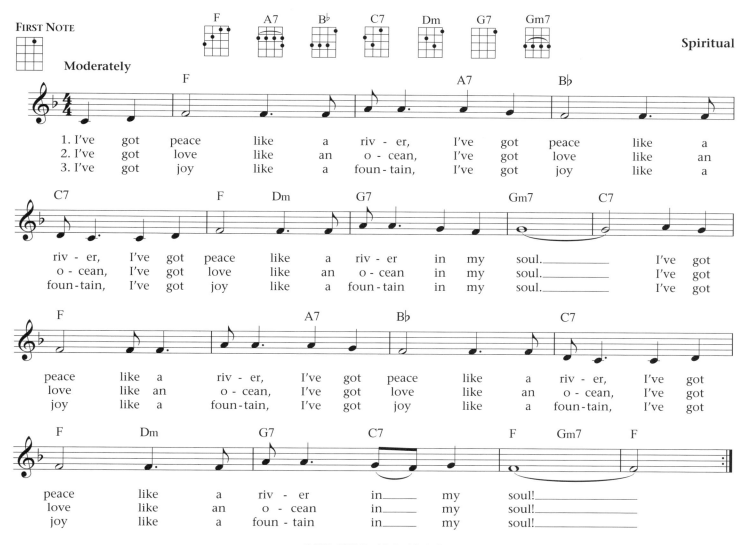

© 2010, 2013 Flea Market Music, Inc.

185

Proud Mary

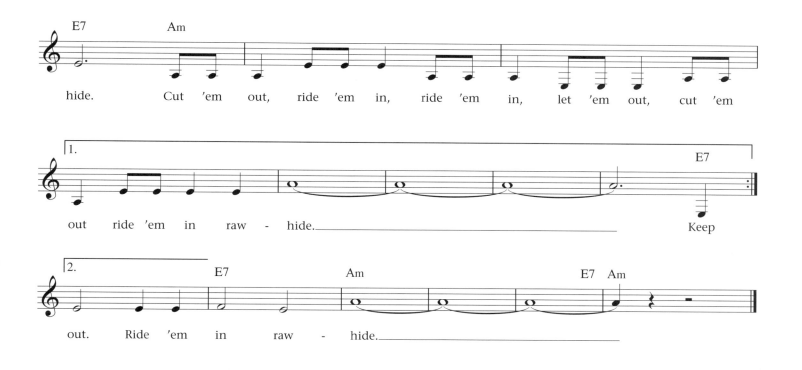

Red River Valley

Traditional American Cowboy Song

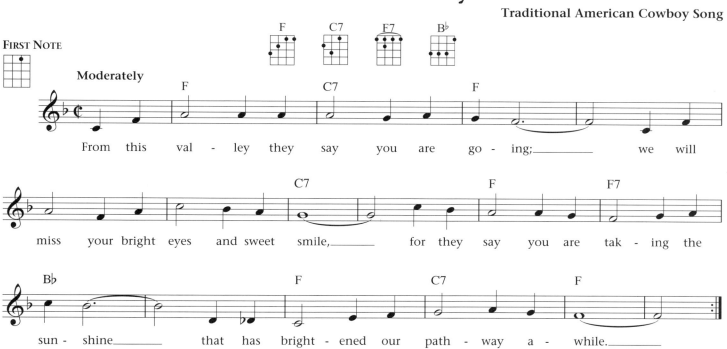

Additional Lyrics

2. Won't you think of this valley you're leaving?
   Oh, how lonely, how sad it will be.
   Oh, think of the fond heart you're breaking
   and the grief you are causing me.

3. Come and sit by my side if you love me.
   Do not hasten to bid me adieu,
   but remember the Red River Valley
   and the cowboy (cowgirl) that loves you so true.

© 2010, 2013 Flea Market Music, Inc.

Seems Like Old Times

Words and Music by JOHN JACOB LOEB and CARMEN LOMBARDO

© 1946 (Renewed 1973) FRED AHLERT MUSIC GROUP (ASCAP)
and FLOJAN MUSIC (ASCAP)/Administered by BUG MUSIC

She Loves You

Words and Music by JOHN LENNON
and PAUL McCARTNEY

She loves you, yeah, yeah, yeah,— she loves you, yeah, yeah, yeah,— she

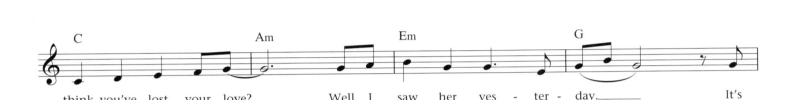

loves you, yeah, yeah, yeah, yeah._____ You

think you've lost your love?__ Well, I saw her yes - ter - day._____ It's

you she's think - ing of__ and she told me what to say._____ She says, she

loves you and you know that can't be bad._____ Yes, she

loves you and you know you should be glad._____ She

said you hurt her so,___ she al - most lost her mind.___ But
know it's up to you,___ I think it's on - ly fair.___

now she says she knows___ you're not the hurt - ing
Pride can hurt you too,___ a - pol - o - gize to

Copyright © 1963 by NORTHERN SONGS LIMITED
Copyright Renewed
All rights for the U.S.A., its territories and possessions and Canada assigned to and controlled by GIL MUSIC CORP., 1650 Broadway, New York, NY 10019

Shall We Gather At The River

Shenandoah

She'll Be Comin' 'Round The Mountain

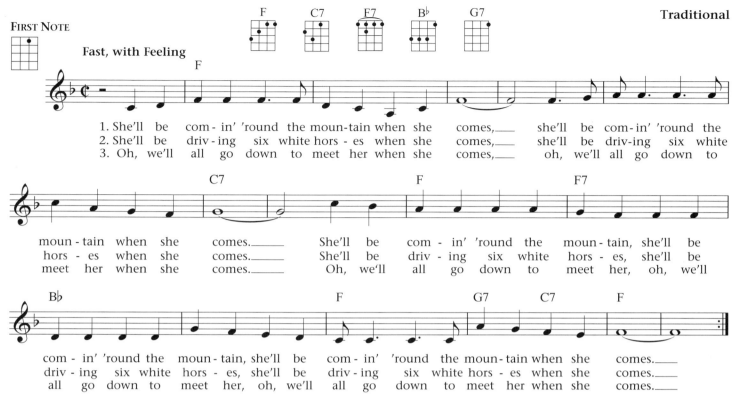

Shine On, Harvest Moon

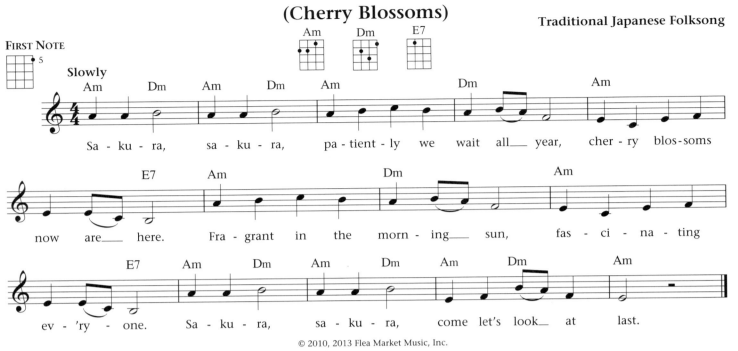

Sidewalks Of New York

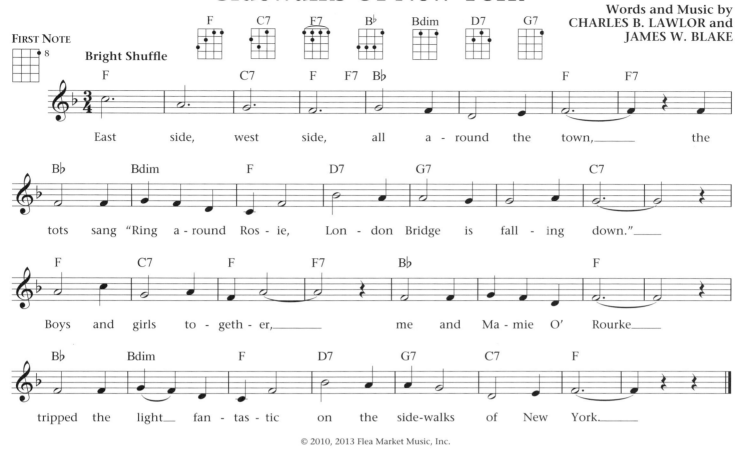

Simple Gifts

The Sloop John B.

Traditional

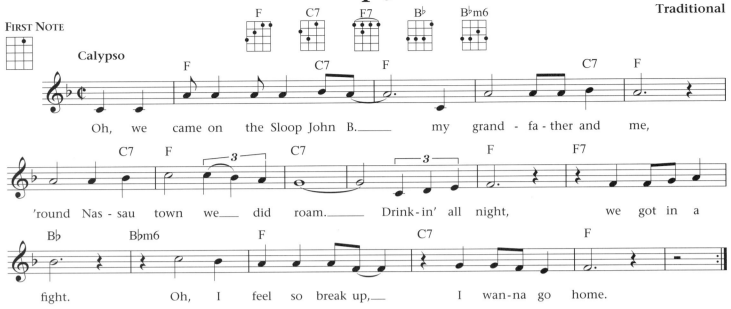

Additional Lyrics

Chorus: (same chords as verse)
So hoist up the John B. sails,
see how the mainsail sets.
Send for the captain ashore, let me go home.
Let me go home, let me go home.
I feel so break up, I wanna go home.

2. The first mate, oh, he got drunk,
broke up the people's trunk,
Constable had to come and take him away.
Sheriff John Stone, please leave me alone.
I feel so break up, I wanna go home.
Chorus

3. The poor cook, oh, he got fits,
throw away all of the grits,
then he took and eat up all of my corn.
Let me go home, I want to go home.
This is the worst trip I've ever been on.
Chorus

© 2010, 2013 Flea Market Music, Inc.

Song Of The Islands

Words and Music by
CHAS. E. KING

© 2010, 2013 Flea Market Music, Inc.

Smiles

Words by J. WILL CALLAHAN
Music by LEE S. ROBERTS

First Note

Liltingly

There are smiles that make us hap-py, there are smiles that make us blue, there are smiles that steal a-way the tear-drops as the sun-beams steal a-way the dew. There are smiles that have a ten-der mean-ing that the eyes of love a-lone may see, and the smiles that fill my life with sun-shine are the smiles that you give to me.

© 2010, 2013 Flea Market Music, Inc.

215

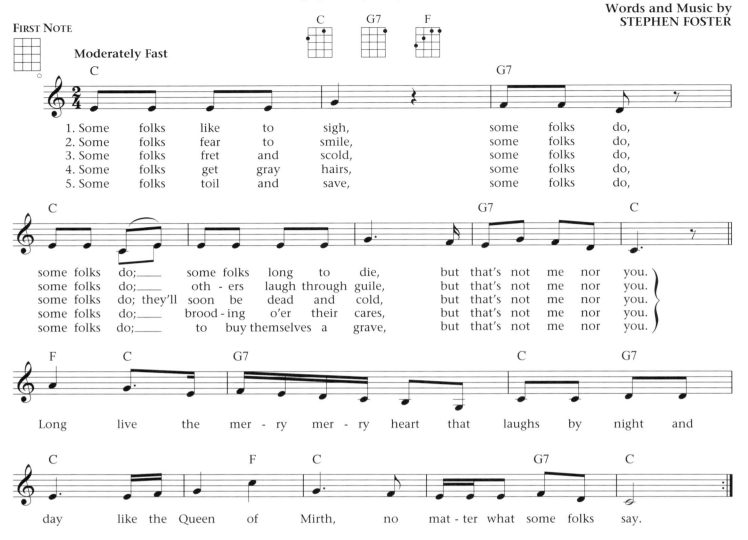

Some Of These Days

Words and Music by
SHELTON BROOKS

Some of these days____ you'll miss__ me, hon-ey,____ some of these

days____ you're gon-na be so lone-ly.____ You'll miss my

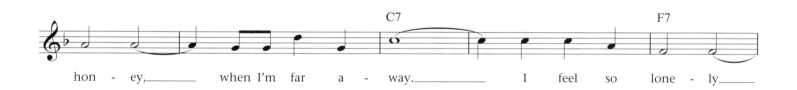

hug-ging,____ you're gon-na miss my kiss-ing,____ you're gon-na miss me

hon-ey,____ when I'm far a-way.____ I feel so lone-ly____

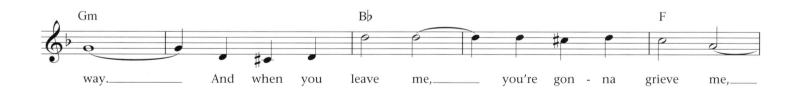

____ for you on-ly,____ 'cause you know, hon-ey,____ you've had your

way.____ And when you leave me,____ you're gon-na grieve me,

____ you'll miss__ your lit-tle ba-by,____ yes, some__ of these days.____

© 2010, 2013 Flea Market Music, Inc.

Stand By Me

Words and Music by JERRY LEIBER, MIKE STOLLER and BEN E. KING

219

The Star Spangled Banner

Words by
FRANCIS SCOTT KEY

Music by
JOHN STAFFORD SMITH

© 2010, 2013 Flea Market Music, Inc.

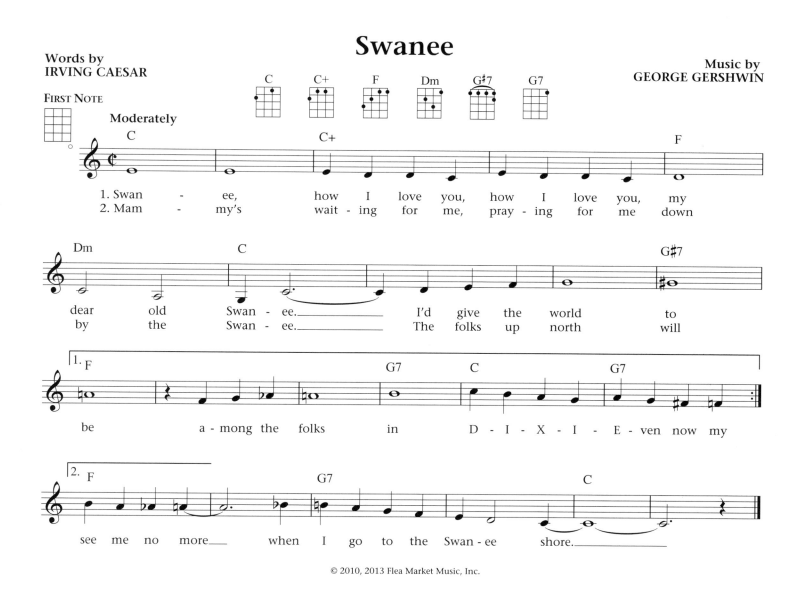

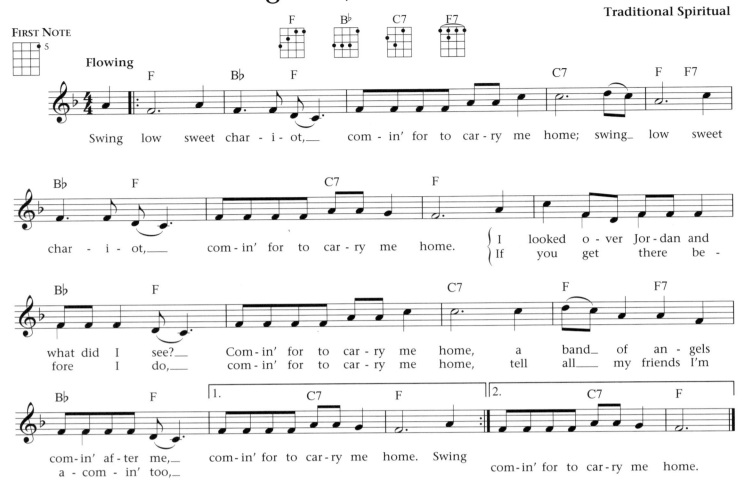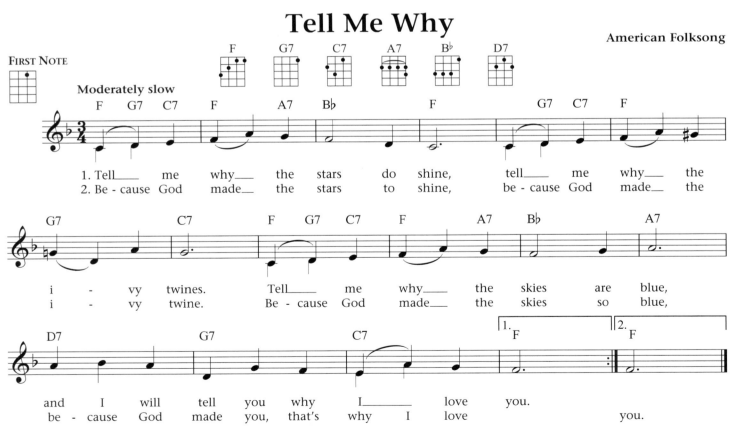

Take Me Out To The Ballgame

Taps

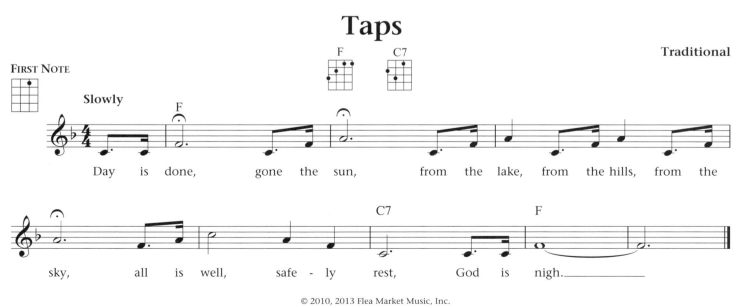

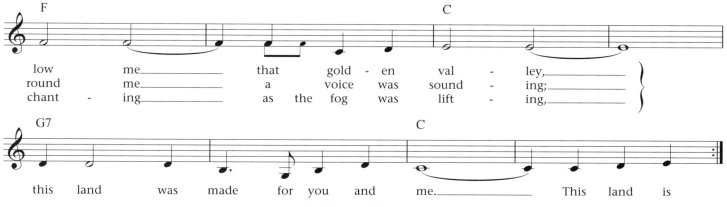

Additional Lyrics

4. In the squares of the cities, by the shadow of the steeples,
   in the relief office, I saw my people.
   And some were stumbling and some were wondering if
   this land was made for you and me.
   Chorus

5. As I went rambling that dusty highway,
   I saw a sign that said, "Private Property."
   But on the other side it didn't say nothing—
   that side was made for you and me.
   Chorus

6. Nobody living can ever stop me,
   as I go walking my freedom highway.
   Nobody living can make me turn back—
   this land was made for you and me.
   Chorus

© 2010, 2013 Flea Market Music, Inc.

235

There Is A Tavern In The Town

Traditional Drinking Song

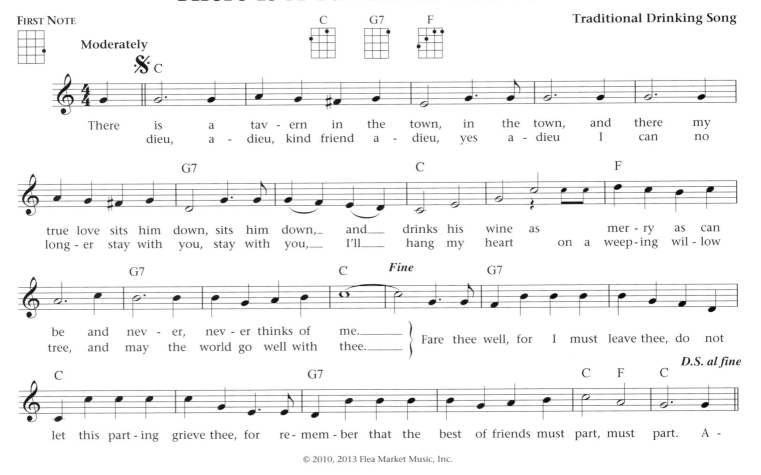

© 2010, 2013 Flea Market Music, Inc.

This Train

Traditional

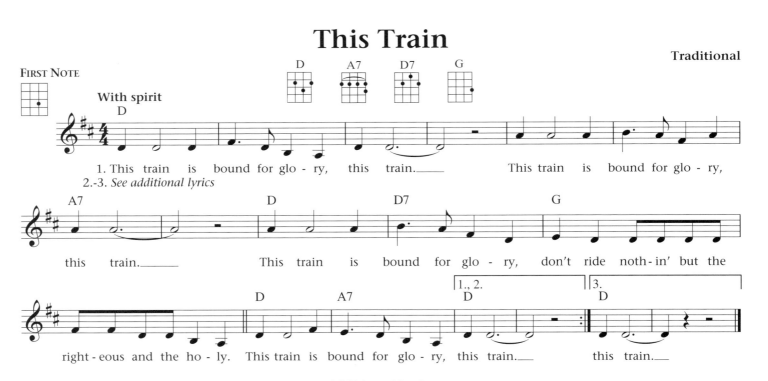

Additional Lyrics

2. This train don't carry no gamblers, this train. (2x)
   This train don't carry no gamblers,
   no hypocrites, no midnight ramblers.
   This train is bound for glory, this train.

3. This train is built for speed now, this train. (2x)
   This train is built for speed now;
   fastest train you ever did see.
   This train is bound for glory, this train.

© 2010, 2013 Flea Market Music, Inc.

The Times They Are A-Changin'

Words and Music by
BOB DYLAN

Additional Lyrics

2. Come writers and critics who prophesize with your pen,
   and keep your eyes wide, the chance won't come again,
   and don't speak too soon for the wheel's still in spin,
   and there's no tellin' who that it's namin',
   for the loser now will be later to win,
   for the times they are a-changin'.

3. Come senators, congressmen, please heed the call
   don't stand in the doorway, don't block up the hall.
   For he that gets hurt will be he who has stalled.
   There's a battle outside and it's ragin'.
   It'll soon shake your windows and rattle your walls,
   for the times they are a-changin'.

4. Come mothers and fathers throughout the land,
   and don't criticize what you can't understand.
   Your sons and your daughters are beyond your command,
   your old road is rapidly agin'.
   Please get out of the new one if you can't lend your hand,
   for the times they are a-changin'.

5. The line it is drawn, the curse it is cast.
   The slow one now will later be fast.
   As the present now will later be past,
   the order is rapidly fadin'.
   And the first one now will later be last,
   for the times they are a-changin'.

Copyright © 1963 Warner Bros. Inc.
Copyright Renewed 1991 Special Rider Music

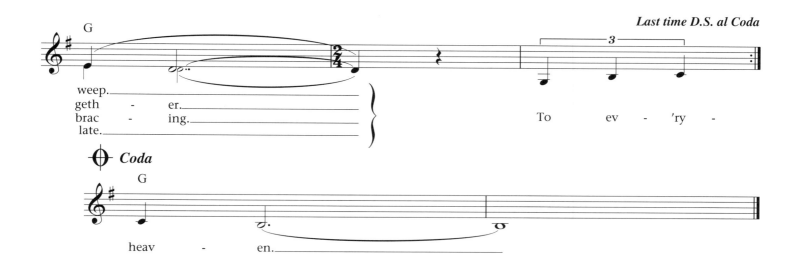

Unchained Melody

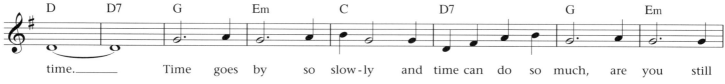

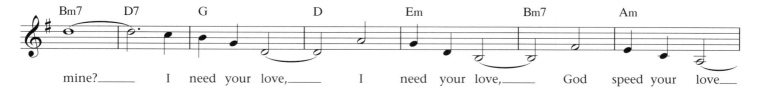

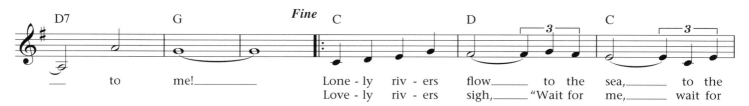

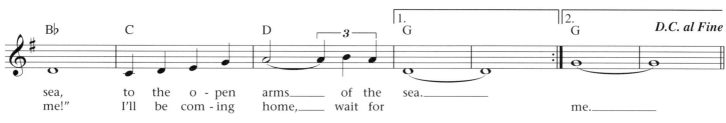

© 1955 (Renewed) FRANK MUSIC CORP.

To You, Sweetheart, Aloha

Ukuleles Are The Best

The Wabash Cannon Ball

Hobo Song

© 2010, 2013 Flea Market Music, Inc.

Wade In The Water

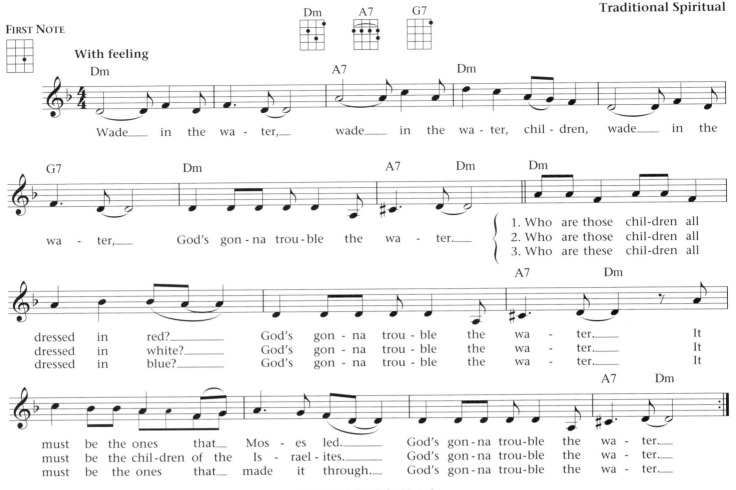

The Water Is Wide

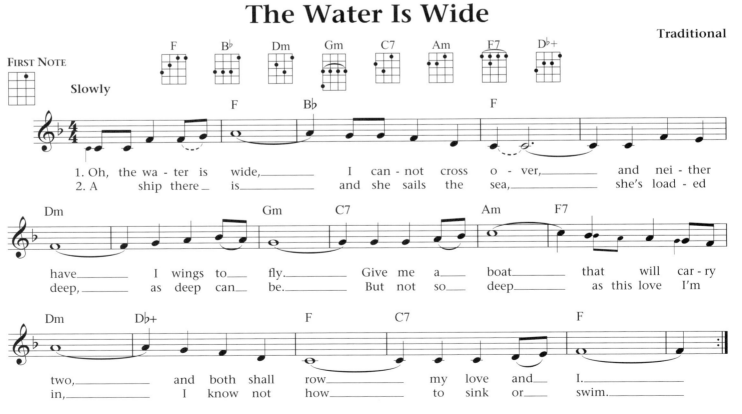

Walk Right In

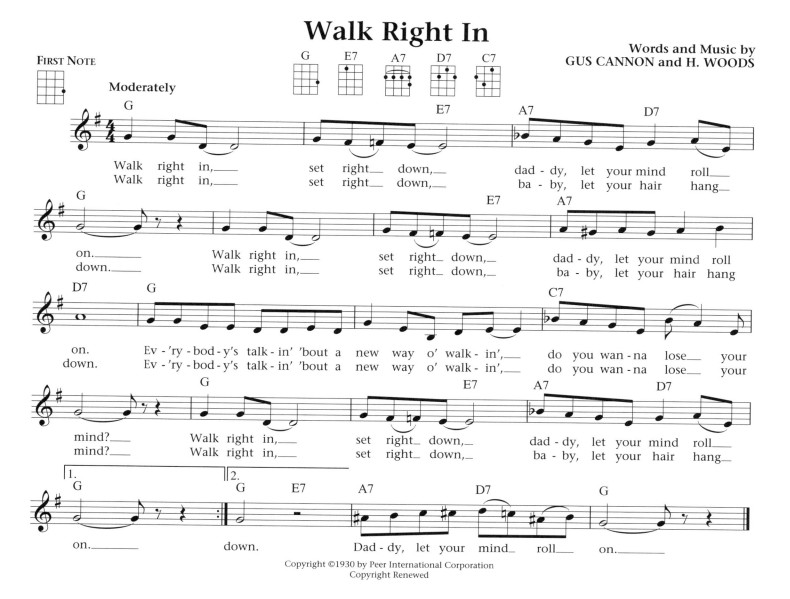

Wayfaring Stranger

We Shall Overcome

Inspired by African American Gospel Singing, members of the Food and Tobacco Workers Union, Charleston, SC and the southern Civil Rights Movement

Musical and Lyrical Adaption by ZILPHIA HORTON, FRANK HAMILTON, GUY CARAWAN, and PETE SEEGER

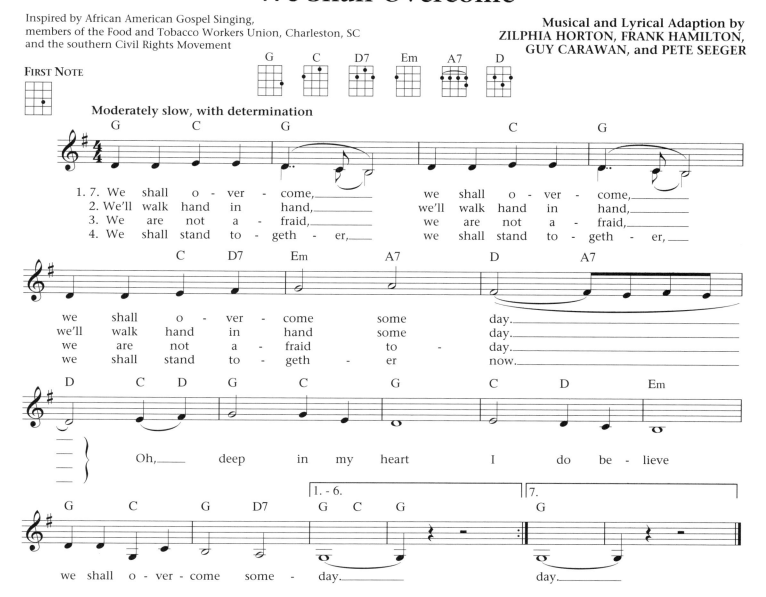

Additional Lyrics

5. The truth will make us free, the truth will make us free,
   the truth will make us free someday, *etc.*

6. We shall live in peace, we shall live in peace,
   we shall live in peace someday, *etc.*

TRO - © Copyright 1960 (Renewed) and 1963 (Renewed) Ludlow Music, Inc., New York, NY

257

What'll I Do?

Words and Music by IRVING BERLIN

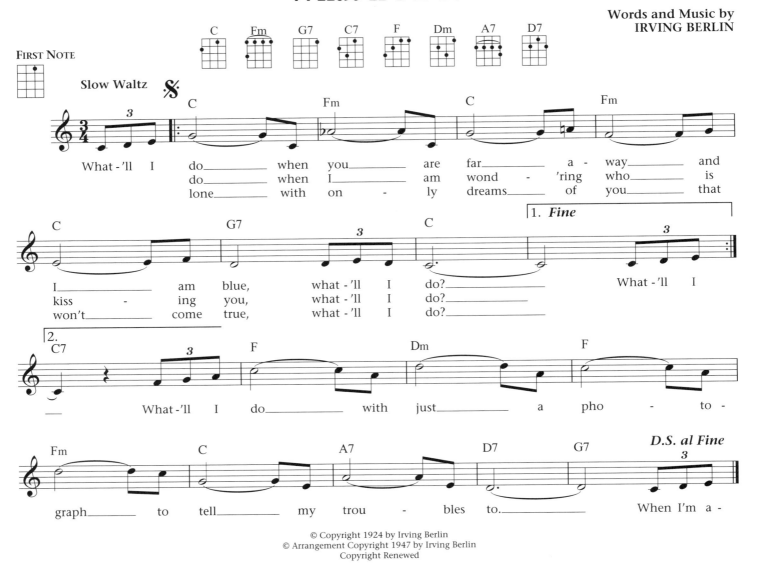

© Copyright 1924 by Irving Berlin
© Arrangement Copyright 1947 by Irving Berlin
Copyright Renewed

When The Red, Red Robin Comes Bob, Bob Bobbin' Along

Words and Music by HARRY WOODS

When the red, red rob-in comes bob, bob bob-bin' a-long, a-long, there'll be no more sob-in', when he starts throb-bin' his old sweet song. Wake up, wake up, you sleep-y-head; get up, get up, get out of bed. Cheer up, cheer up, the sun is red, live, love, laugh and be hap-py. What if I've been blue, now I'm walk-in' through fields of flow'rs. Rain may glis-ten, but still I lis-ten for hours and hours. I'm just a kid a-gain, do-in' what I did a-gain, sing-ing a song, when the red, red rob-in comes bob, bob bob-bin' a-long.

Copyright © 1926 CALLICOON MUSIC
Copyright Renewed
All Rights Administered by THE SONGWRITERS GUILD OF AMERICA

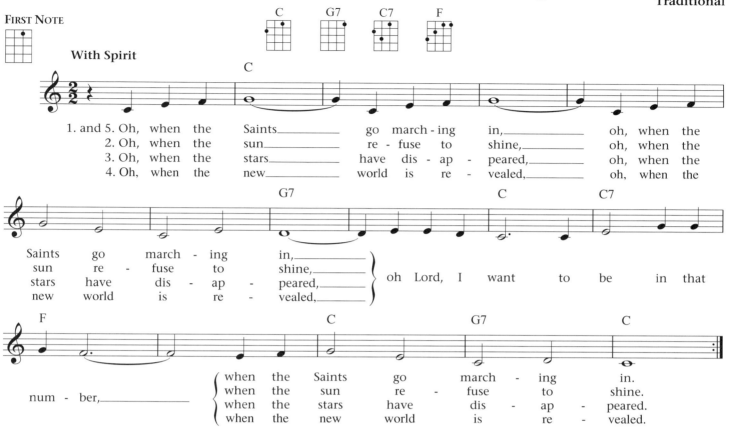
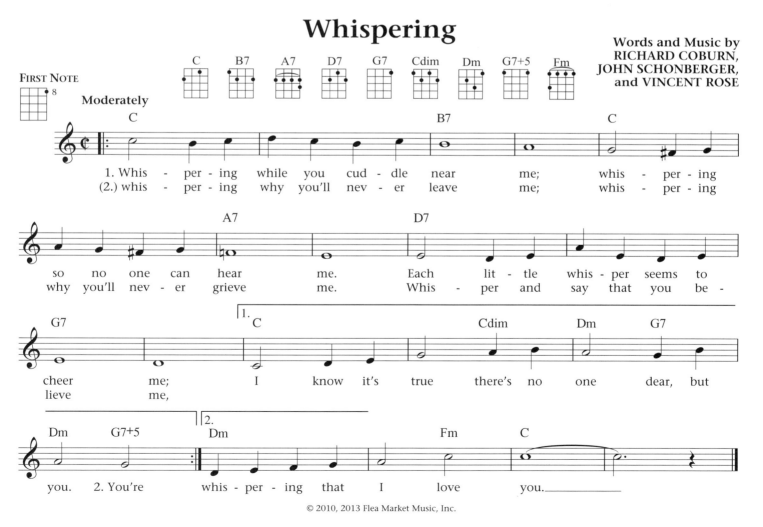

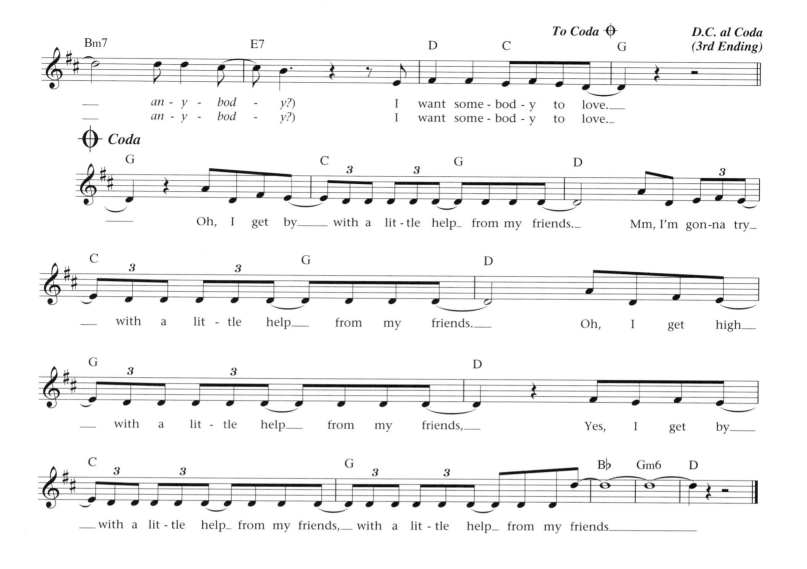

The World Is Waiting For The Sunrise

Words by
EUGENE LOCKHART

Music by
ERNEST SEITZ

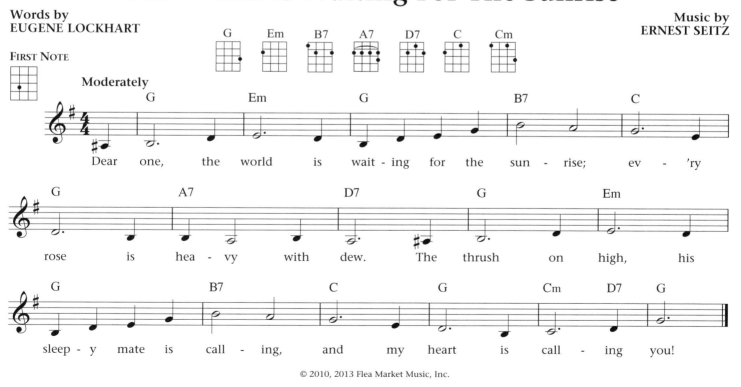

© 2010, 2013 Flea Market Music, Inc.

The Yellow Rose Of Texas

Traditional

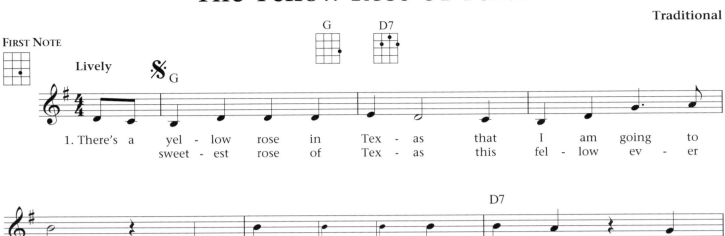

Additional Lyrics

3. Where the Rio Grande is flowing
   and starry nights are bright,
   she walks along the river
   each quiet summer night.
   She thinks of when we parted
   so very long ago;
   I promised I would come back,
   no more to leave her so.
   Chorus

4. Now I'm goin' back to find her,
   my heart is full of woe.
   We'll sing the songs that we used
   to sing so long ago.
   I'll play the banjo gaily,
   we'll sing forever more;
   the yellow rose of Texas,
   the girl that I adore.
   Chorus

© 2010, 2013 Flea Market Music, Inc.

Songs For
Holidays and Celebrations

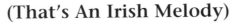
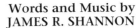
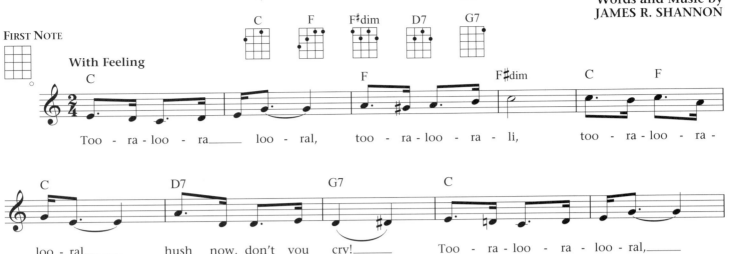
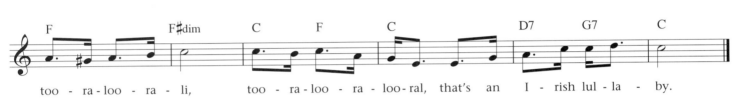

Anniversary Song

Words and Music by
AL JOLSON and SAUL CHAPLIN

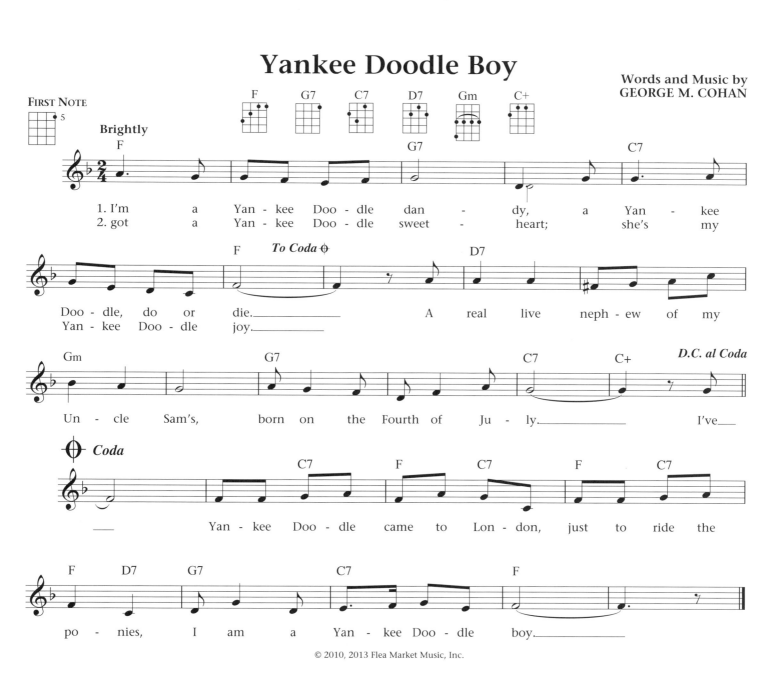

Over The River And Through The Woods

Words by
LYDIA MARIA CHILD

Traditional

Additional Lyrics

2. Over the river and through the woods
   to have a first-rate play.
   Oh, hear the bells ring: "ting-a-ling ling."
   Hurrah for Thanksgiving Day.
   Over the river and through the woods,
   trot fast, my dapple gray.
   Spring o'er the ground like hunting hound,
   for this is Thanksgiving Day!

3. Over the river and through the woods,
   and straight through the barnyard gate.
   We seem to go extremely slow,
   it is so hard to wait.
   Over the river and through the woods,
   now grandmother's cap I spy.
   Hurrah for fun, the pudding's done!
   Hurrah for the pumpkin pie!

© 2010, 2013 Flea Market Music, Inc.

Prayer Of Thanksgiving

Traditional

With Reverence

1. We gath-er to-geth-er to ask the Lord's bless-ing, He chas-tens and has-tens His will to make known. The wick-ed op-press-ing cease them from dis-tress-ing, sing prais-es to His name, He for-gets not His own.
2. Be-side us to guide us, our God with us join-ing, or-dain-ing, main-tain-ing His King-dom di-vine. So, from the be-gin-ning, the fight we were win-ning, the Lord, is at our side, the glo-ry di-vine.
3. We all do ex-tol thee, thou lead-er in bat-tle, and pray that thou still our de-fend-er will be. Let thy con-gre-ga-tion es-cape trib-u-la-tion, thy name be ev-er praised! O, Lord make us free.

© 2010, 2013 Flea Market Music, Inc.

293

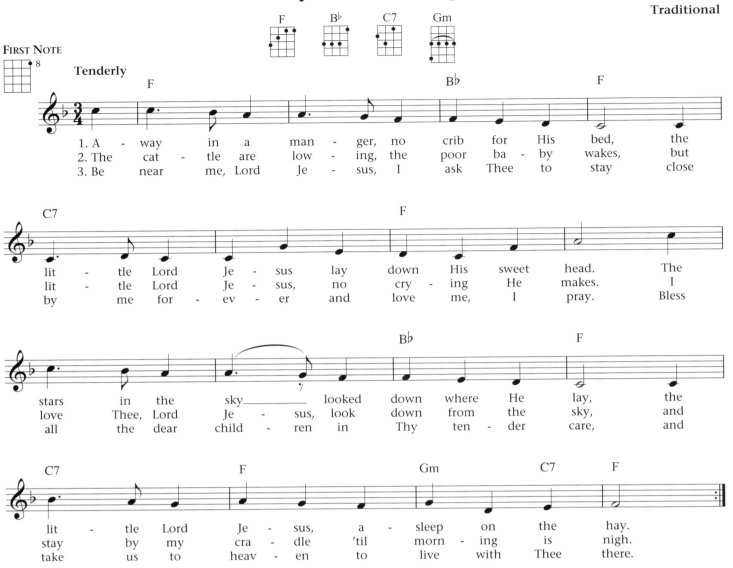

Blue Christmas

Words and Music by BILLY HAYES and JAY JOHNSON

I'll have a blue Christ-mas, with-out you. I'll be so blue think-ing a-bout you. Dec-o-ra-tions of red on a green Christ-mas tree won't mean a thing if you're not here with me. I'll have a

blue Christ-mas, that's cer-tain. And when that blue heart-ache starts hurt-in', you'll be do-in' all right with your Christ-mas of

white, but I'll have a blue, blue Christ-mas

Copyright © 1948 UNIVERSAL - POLYGRAM INTERNATIONAL PUBLISHING, INC. and Judy J. Olmstead Trust
Copyright Renewed
All Rights for JUDY J. OLMSTEAD TRUST Controlled and Administered by LICHELLE MUSIC COMPANY

297

The Chipmunk Song

Words and Music by
ROSS BAGDASARIAN

Christ - mas, Christ - mas time is near, time for toys and time for cheer. We've been good but we can't last, hur - ry Christ - mas, hur - ry fast! Want a plane that loops the loop; me, I want a hu - la hoop. We can hard - ly stand the wait, please Christ - mas, don't be late.

Copyright © 1958 Bagdasarian Productions LLC
Copyright Renewed

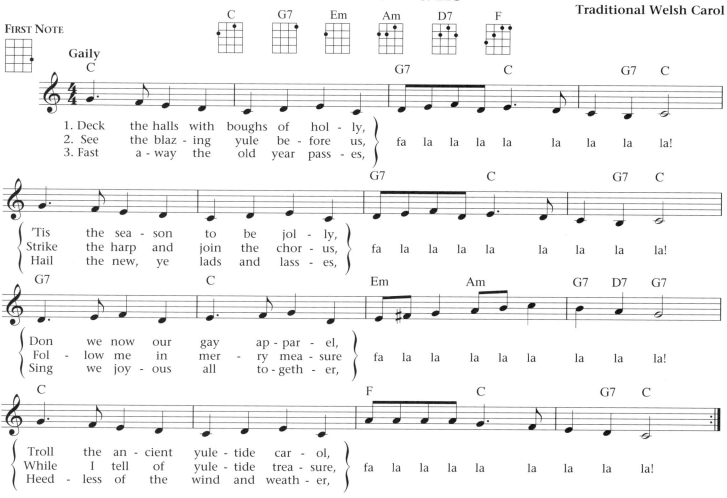

The First Noel

17th Century English Carol

Additional Lyrics

3. And by the light of that same star,
   three wise men came from country far;
   to seek for a King was their intent,
   and to follow the star wherever it went.
   (Chorus)

© 2010, 2013 Flea Market Music, Inc.

301

# Joy To The World

Additional Lyrics

3. No more let sins and sorrows grow,
   nor thorns infest the ground.
   He comes to make His blessings flow
   far as the curse is found.
   Far as the curse is found,
   far as, far as the curse is found.

4. He rules the world with truth and grace,
   and makes the nations prove
   the glories of His righteousness
   and wonders of His love.
   And wonders of His love,
   and wonders, wonders of His love.

O Come, All Ye Faithful
(Adeste Fideles)

Latin Words Translated by
FREDERICK OAKELEY

Music by
JOHN FRANCIS WADE

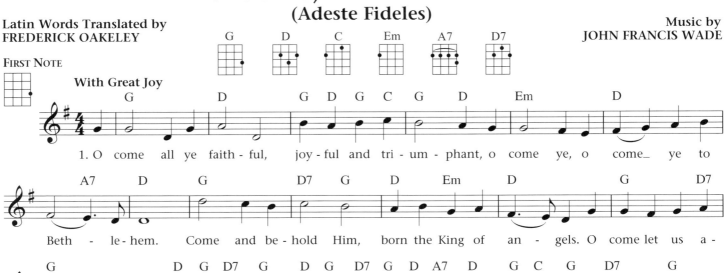

Additional Lyrics

2. Sing, choirs of angels,
sing in exultation,
sing, all ye citizens of heaven above:
Glory to God,
glory in the highest!
Refrain

3. Yes, Lord, we greet thee,
born this happy morning,
Jesus, to Thee be glory given.
Word of the Father,
now in flesh appearing.
Refrain

© 2010, 2013 Flea Market Music, Inc.

Silent Night

Words by **JOSEPH MÖHR**
Translated by **JOHN F. YOUNG**

Music by
FRANZ X. GRUBER

3. Silent night, Holy night,
Son of God, love's pure light.
Radiant beams from thy holy face,
with the dawn of redeeming grace,
Jesus, Lord at thy birth.
Jesus, Lord at thy birth.

© 2010, 2013 Flea Market Music, Inc.

Songs For Children

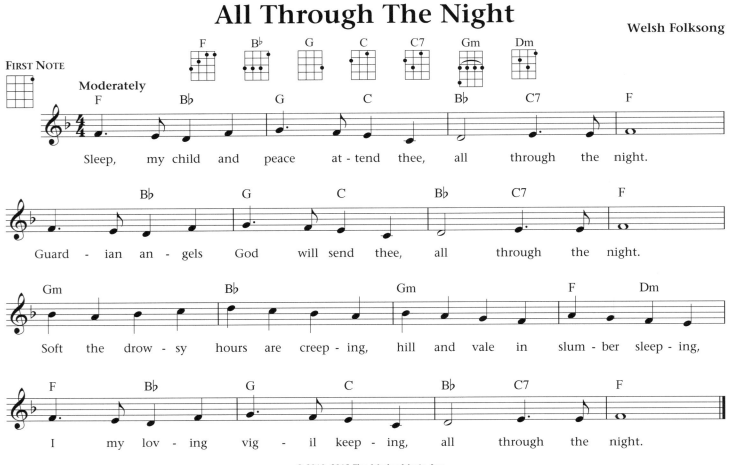

Alphabet Song

Baa, Baa, Black Sheep

The Bear Went Over The Mountain

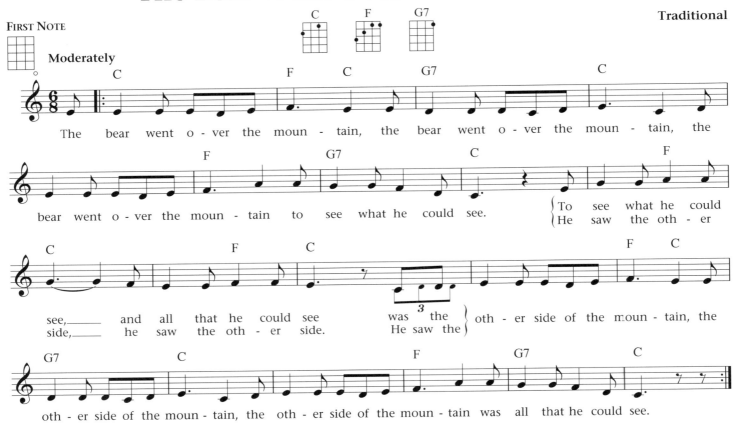

Brahms' Lullaby

The Candy Man

Words and Music by LESLIE BRICUSSE and ANTHONY NEWLEY

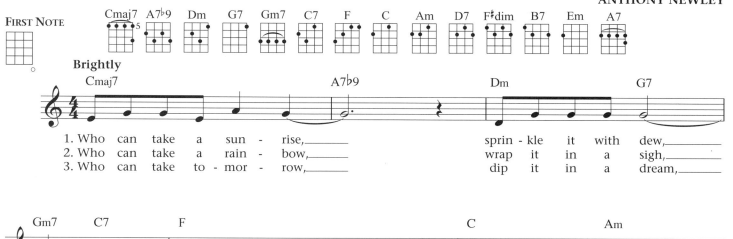

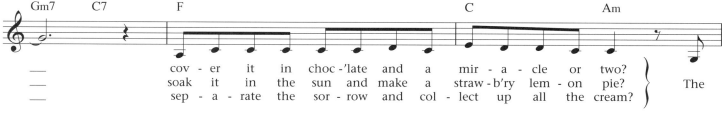

1. Who can take a sun - rise, sprin - kle it with dew,
2. Who can take a rain - bow, wrap it in a sigh,
3. Who can take to - mor - row, dip it in a dream,

— cov - er it in choc - 'late and a mir - a - cle or two?
— soak it in the sun and make a straw - b'ry lem - on pie? } The
— sep - a - rate the sor - row and col - lect up all the cream?

Can - dy Man, the Can - dy Man can. The

Can - dy Man can, 'cause he mix - es it with love and makes the world taste good.

1. *2., 3. Fine*

The Can - dy Man makes ev - 'ry - thing he bakes

sat - is - fy - ing and de - li - cious. Talk a - bout your child - hood

D.C. al Fine

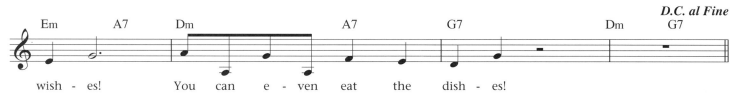

wish - es! You can e - ven eat the dish - es!

Copyright © 1970, 1971 by Taradam Music, Inc.
Copyright Renewed

Do-Re-Mi

Lyrics by
OSCAR HAMMERSTEIN II

Music by
RICHARD RODGERS

Copyright © 1959 by Richard Rodgers and Oscar Hammerstein II
Copyright Renewed
WILLIAMSON MUSIC owner of publication and allied rights throughout the world

Eensy Weensy Spider

Traditional

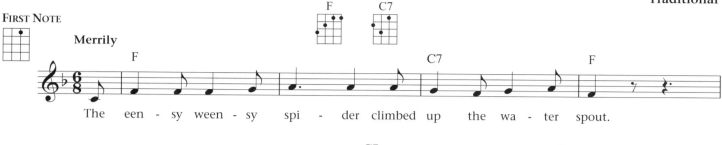

© 2010, 2013 Flea Market Music, Inc.

The Farmer In The Dell

Traditional

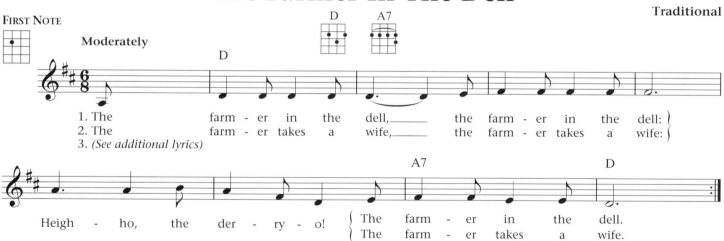

Additional Lyrics

3. The wife takes a child,
   the wife takes a child:
   Heigh-ho, the derry-o!
   The wife takes a child.

4. The child takes a nurse,
   the child takes a nurse:
   Heigh-ho, the derry-o!
   The child takes a nurse.

5. The nurse takes a cow,
   the nurse takes a cow:
   Heigh-ho, the derry-o!
   The nurse takes a cow.

6. The cow takes a dog,
   the cow takes a dog:
   Heigh-ho, the derry-o!
   The cow takes a dog.

7. The dog takes a cat,
   the dog takes a cat:
   Heigh-ho, the derry-o!
   The dog takes a cat.

8. The cat takes a rat,
   the cat takes a rat:
   Heigh-ho, the derry-o!
   The cat takes a rat.

9. The rat takes the cheese,
   the rat takes the cheese:
   Heigh-ho, the derry-o!
   The rat takes the cheese.

10. The cheese stands alone,
    the cheese stands alone:
    Heigh-ho, the derry-o!
    The cheese stands alone.

© 2010, 2013 Flea Market Music, Inc.

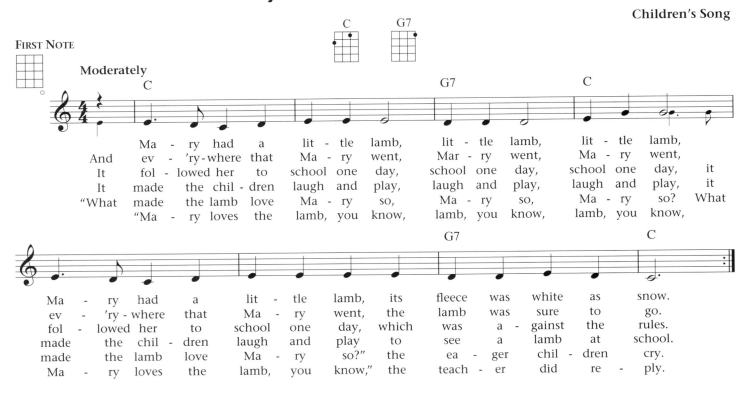

Mickey Mouse March

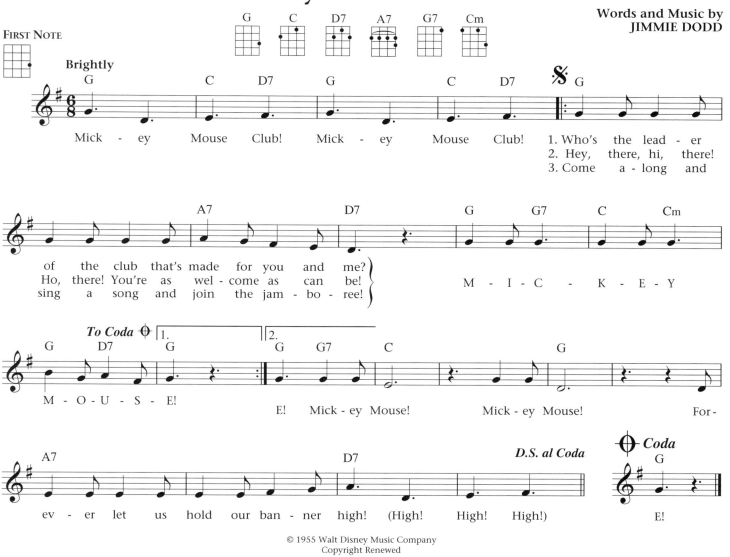

© 1955 Walt Disney Music Company
Copyright Renewed

Oh Where, Oh Where Has My Little Dog Gone?

© 2010, 2013 Flea Market Music, Inc.

321

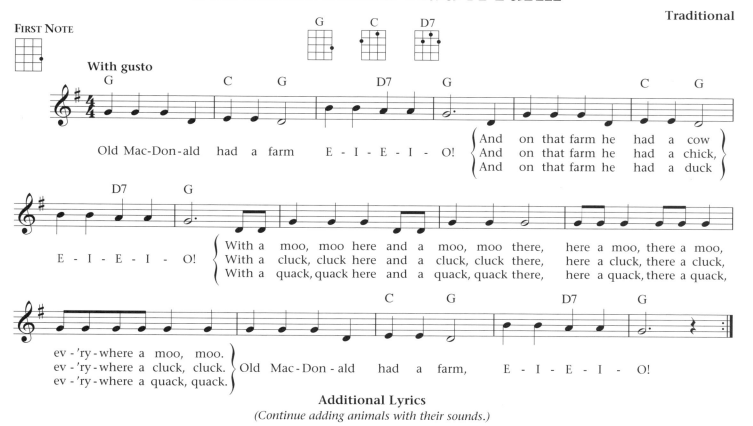
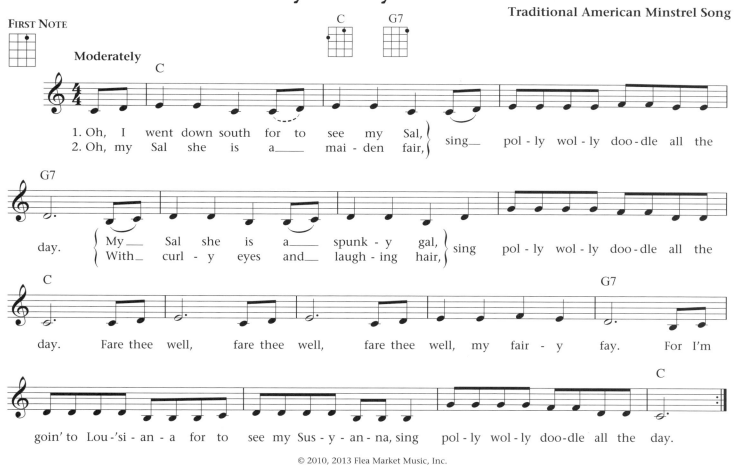

Row, Row, Row Your Boat

Traditional

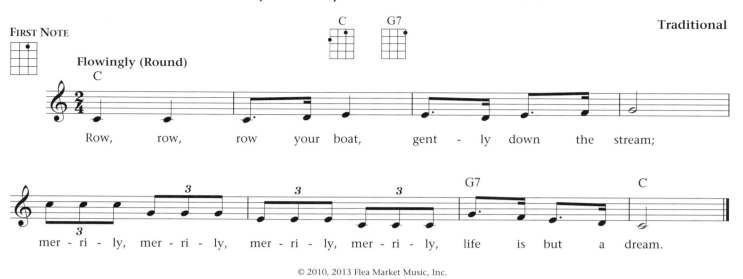

Skip To My Lou

Traditional

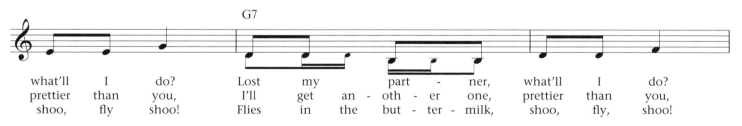

This Old Man

Traditional

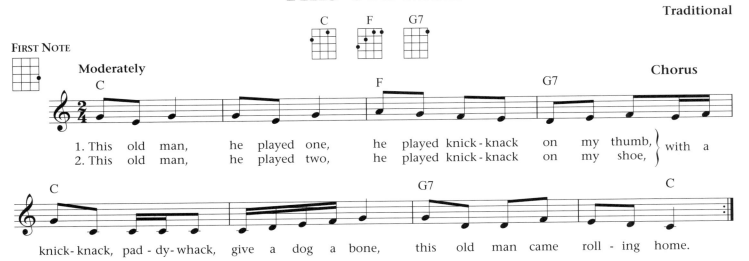

Additional Lyrics

3. This old man, he played three,
   he played knick-knack on my knee.
   Chorus

4. This old man, he played four,
   he played knick-knack on my door.
   Chorus

5. This old man, he played five,
   he played knick-knack on my hive.
   Chorus

6. This old man, he played six,
   he played knick-knack on my sticks.
   Chorus

7. This old man, he played seven,
   he played knick-knack up to heaven.
   Chorus

8. This old man, he played eight,
   he played knick-knack on my gate.
   Chorus

9. This old man, he played nine,
   he played knick-knack on my vine.
   Chorus

10. This old man, he played ten,
    he played knick-knack over again.
    Chorus

© 2010, 2013 Flea Market Music, Inc.

Three Blind Mice

Traditional

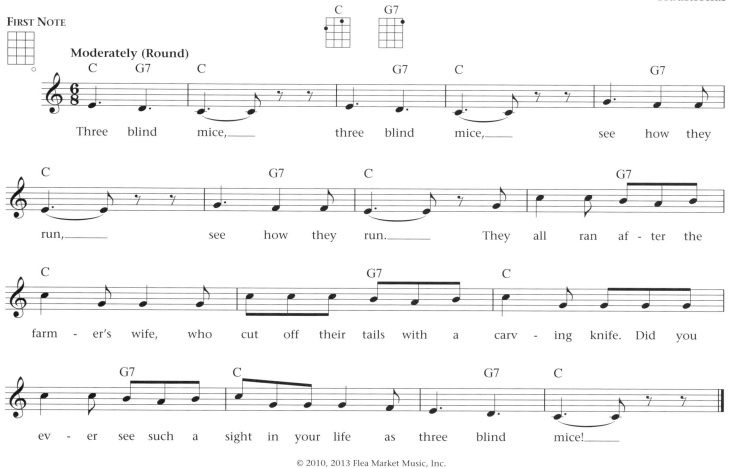

© 2010, 2013 Flea Market Music, Inc.

Twinkle, Twinkle Little Star

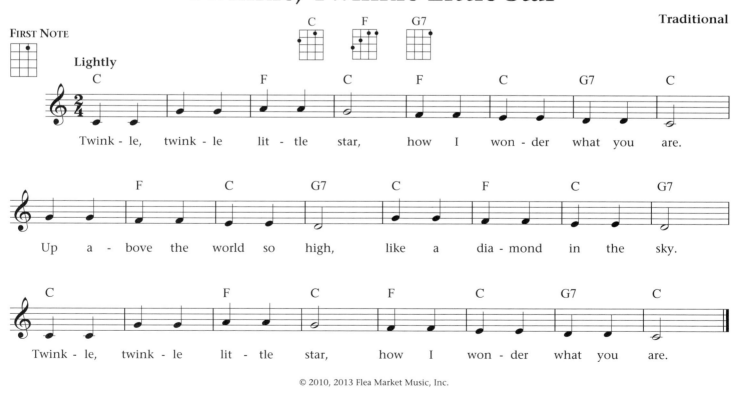

© 2010, 2013 Flea Market Music, Inc.

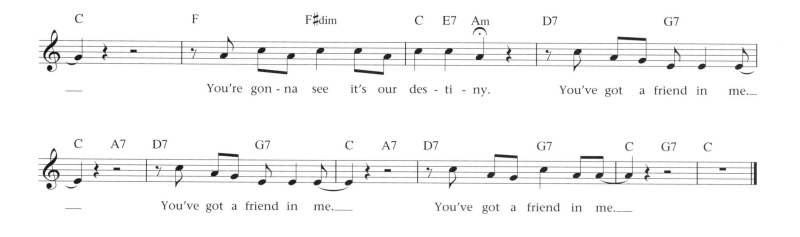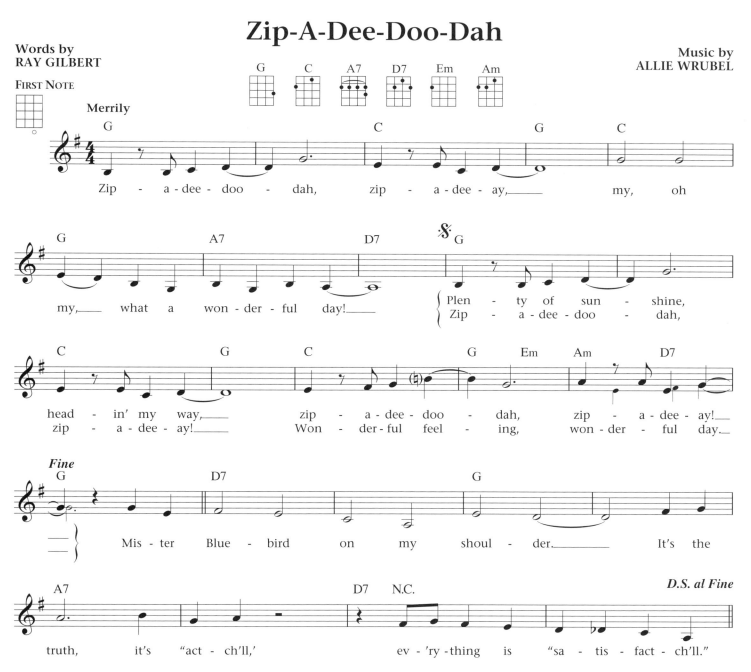

Your Notes Here

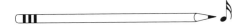

Your Notes Here

Thank You

Our biggest thank you goes to Ronny Schiff and Charylu Roberts, both of whom have been part of the team since the very first *Jumpin' Jim's* songbook. Also, major thanks to Jeff Schroedl, Dan Bauer, Jerry Muccio, David Jahnke, David Dinan, Denis Kavemeier, Trish Dulka, Lori Hagopian, Larry Morton, Keith Mardak and everyone else at Hal Leonard Corp. for your enormous help in making this songbook a reality. Finally, thank you to all who suggested songs or helped in one way or another to make this book what it is, especially: Tony Cappa, Andy Andrews, Peter Thomas, Pete McDonnell, Rick Scanlan, Geoff Rezek, Mike and Marv Beloff, Liz Drouin, Eileen Schiess, Jim Rosokoff, John and Evelyn Chandler, Lionel Cranfield, Fred Sokolow, Phil Rosenthal, Tim Mann, Lil' Rev, Pete Zaccagnino, Shirley Davis, Shirley Orlando, Susan McCormick, Paul Cundari, Doug Haverty, Steve Boisen, Tom Favilla, Kathy Sumpter, Ella Jenkins, Bernadelle Richter, Cathy Fink, Marcy Marxer and Cybill Shepherd. And you!

Liz and Jim Beloff

Finding a ukulele at the Pasadena Rose Bowl Flea Market in 1992 inspired Liz and Jim Beloff to start Flea Market Music, Inc., publisher of the popular *Jumpin' Jim's* series of ukulele songbooks including *The Daily Ukulele: 365 Songs For Better Living* and *The Daily Ukulele: Leap Year Edition*.

Jim Beloff is the author of *The Ukulele—A Visual History* (1997, Backbeat Books), producer of *Legends of Ukulele*, a CD compilation for Rhino Records and has made three how-to-play DVDs for Homespun Tapes, *The Joy of Uke #1* and *#2* and *Jumpin' Jim's Ukulele Workshop*. He is also an active songwriter who has collaborated and recorded with ukulele legends, Herb Ohta (Ohta-San) and Lyle Ritz.

Liz Maihock Beloff, with a background in film and television graphics, designs the covers and art-directs all of FMM's songbooks, CDs and DVDs. Having been weaned on *The Lawrence Welk Show* in her Midwestern early childhood, she has a remarkable recall of American popular music. She is also a talented singer who, before teaming up with Jim, sang with *a cappella* groups in college and New York City.

Jim and Liz regularly perform together at ukulele events playing the unique Fluke, Flea and Firefly ukuleles manufactured by The Magic Fluke Co. They truly believe in their company's motto, "Uke Can Change the World." You can reach them through the Flea Market Music web site at: www.fleamarketmusic.com.

Rick Scanlan Photography